Supernatural Survival Guide

Laura Powers

Copyright © 2016

Cover Photo or design by Penny O Photography

All rights reserved. This book may not be reproduced in whole or in part, or transmitted in any form, without the written permission from the publisher except by a reviewer who may quote brief passages in review.

Library of Congress Data Available Upon Request

ISBN 978-0-9975087-5-8

First Printing, October 2016

Dedication

This book is dedicated to Jared Padalecki and Jensen Ackles, a.k.a. Sam and Dean Winchester, and those who bring the show *Supernatural* to life. I love seeing the supernatural world depicted in an often light-hearted way! I am glad that shows like this are getting people to talk and think about the supernatural world and how it mingles with the human world, even if shows like this are doing it in a fictitious way.

Acknowledgements

I would like to acknowledge all those accused of witchcraft, who were burned at the stake and who were wrongly tortured and killed. I am thankful to be living in a time and place where someone with my gifts can make a living and be appreciated for their gifts instead of being ostracized, hurt, or worse. For those who have gifts and are afraid to come forward, know that the more of us who do, the easier it is for those with gifts to feel comfortable and safe with who they are.

Special Thanks

Special thanks to Christine Lunday, formerly from deVour Magazine, as well as Kevin Warn and makeup artist Natalie Kameroglu. Thank you also to Cheri Wilson Chagollan of Wonderland Studios for the fabulous wardrobe we used for the photoshoot. Thank you to my mother Christine Webb for her keen eye for details, her inspiration and support. Thank you to Penny O Photography for the cover layout and design! Thank you to all of my wonderful fans and supporters, I couldn't do this without you.

Table of Contents

Dedication 3

Acknowledgements i

Special Thanks ii

Introduction 1

ONE Angels 7

TWO Ghosts 13

THREE Demons and Dark Entities 19

FOUR Faeries 30

FIVE Dragons 39

SIX Vampires 45

SEVEN Werewolves 54

EIGHT Hunters 59

NINE Witches 64

TEN Devil(s) 69

ELEVEN Fallen Angels 73

TWELVE Djinn 81

THIRTEEN Zombies 95

Afterword 101

Helpful Terms/Glossary 102

Recommended Resources/Reading List 110

Sources 119

About the Author – Laura Powers 134

Introduction

I initially wrote this as an article for the October edition of *deVour Magazine* in 2015. I was so interested and excited about the topic that I decided to flesh it out significantly and turn it into a complete book. I decided to do this because I love the topic and it is so appropriate for Halloween, but also because I did not know of any books that had the information I wanted to share. While this book can be read purely for entertainment purposes, my intention is that the guidance, tips, and suggestions will have some practical application as well. I realize that much of what I say in here may be hard for people to swallow. I am telling you that the creatures I am writing about (except for zombies) are real supernatural creatures that you might run into. While human interactions with some of these beings are rare, they are more common than you think and there is a specific set of rules and protection techniques and recommendations that differ from supernatural being to supernatural being. So whether you are reading this book for fun or to learn, I hope you get something out of it. While I do recommend reading chapter one on angels first, after that you can feel free to jump around or read sequentially as your heart desires. I suggest reading the chapter on angels first because they are great at protecting us from a whole host of dangers, so learning about them first is smart and safe.

While it might be frightening to think about these beings interacting with us, know that they have been here on earth for as long or almost as long as humans, and some of them precede us. The idea that vampires, werewolves, and shapeshifters are walking around with us might be terrifying to some. I feel that being educated is actually the first step to learning how to be safe. I also want others to know that most of these beings (aside from demons, devils, dark entities, and fallen angels) are similar to humans in that they can be light or dark or, more likely, gray. There are humans who are saints, like Mother Theresa, and those who are serial killers. Those of extreme light and dark can be found in other species as well. Each individual may be light, dark or somewhere in the middle. Demons, devils, dark entities, and fallen angels are purely dark, however, and I don't recommend giving them a chance or ever hearing them out. Their influence will only bring about pain, destruction, and darkness.

In terms of the release date of this book, Halloween time is the season for specters, ghouls, vampires, werewolves, zombies and things that go bump in the night. There is a reason we celebrate Halloween at the end of October and not the beginning of May. The veil between the world of the living and the world of the dead is the thinnest in late October and early November in the northern hemisphere. Cultures all over the world celebrate this. In the United States, we celebrate this as Halloween and other celebrations include Samhain, All Souls Day, and Dia de Los Muertos (Day of the Dead), amongst others. This can be a wonderfully spooky time of year that can bring fun and laughter but chills and fear as well. They fall during the sign of Scorpio which is all about the hidden or the unexpressed, so I believe that is part of why the veil is the thinnest during this time. It is time for that which is hidden and normally invisible to be seen.

This is the perfect time to share some practical tips for what to do if you encounter a spirit or something supernatural during this very magical and mysterious part of the year. Some of the creatures and beings that I talk about are considered myth or make-believe. I am here to tell you that some of them are not. I am not telling you this to scare you or make you nervous. There truly is a struggle between the light and dark forces in the world. It is happening in the world all around us and one of the main weapons the dark side uses is fear. By learning how to handle something, we can reduce or eliminate our fear and improve our chances of survival and success. The same is true in the physical world. When you encounter a mountain lion, there are certain tactics that work better than others. Understanding these tactics can help you survive. Those uneducated about mountain lion encounters might turn around and run, thereby engaging the animal's chase instinct, a sure-fire way to get attacked. Those knowledgeable will make themselves as large looking as possible (arms in the air and stand up tall) while simultaneously backing away. The difference between these two reactions can mean the difference between life and death.

While you are unlikely to be actually killed by anything I discuss here, some of these beings can make your life tougher and less pleasant. Besides, even though some of this stuff sounds scary, wouldn't you rather be a part of the magic world than the muggle world? The magical world has much to offer. Yes, there are dementors and "he who shall not be named", but also there are unicorns, dragons, and house gnomes. While the muggle world can be safe, I much prefer the excitement of the world of magic. Whatever your preference, remembering these tools and tips could help you when you are in a bind, even if you prefer the muggle world, and the magical world and the mundane world often intermingle.

So read these tips as entertainment or read them for practical use. I come by my knowledge from life experience and professional experience as a psychic medium, ghost whisperer, demon clearer, and general adventurer. I have loved, been friends with, fought with, and been terrified by some of these beings myself. I won't be sharing the details here, but let's just say the stories are juicy. Below, I share general explanations of each type of being and suggestions and tips on how to protect yourself. Also if you understand the patterns and signs of each different type of being, it allows you to protect yourself more effectively.

Some of the beings I write about here are physical creatures, some are extradimensional, and some are both. Extradimensional means that they are from another dimension or parallel universe and have the ability to come to ours. This is different than the term extraterrestrial which refers to a being not from our plane or dimension but from a different terra, or planet. That said, I find that there is a lot of confusion between what may be extradimensional and what is extraterrestrial. This is understandable since when we encounter something we are not likely to enquire or be able to determine whether they are extradimensional or extraterrestrial. In each section, I will describe whether they are from this plane or not and give tips for managing and understanding each type of being.

I've written this book so that you can get a snapshot and real tips on dealing with and protecting yourself from supernatural creatures by reading the summation at the beginning of each chapter. If you want to dig deeper on each type of being, you can read the stories and longer messages in the chapter.

P.S. Though I have titled this book the *Supernatural Survival Guide*, do know that there are light and dark beings in many forms. It is possible to have a light vampire and a dark faerie. Use your judgement but also do not discriminate against form alone. That said, sometimes protection is necessary and learning how different beings operate can be very helpful and also entertaining.

So whether you are reading this for practical purposes or for fun, I hope you enjoy it. Happy reading!

P.S. Halloween is wonderful because it gives many non-human creatures the opportunity to hide in plain sight. Don't be too surprised if some of the exceptional costumes you see during Halloween season, are not costumes at all!

The supernatural is the natural not yet understood.

~Elbert Hubbard

ONE
Angels

Other names: The Messengers, the Watchers

What are they? Angels are beings made of light and love. They are neither animal nor human and although our loved ones can act as our angels, generally speaking, people are people and angels are angels. Angels are tasked by the creator with protecting and assisting humanity, animals, and other life forces. They do that by guiding us, providing loving support, and intervening when we are off our path and need help. There are many types of angels, from angels the size of galaxies to relatively small angels that help us. Though they are made of energy, they can also manifest and create matter and physical form which includes their own bodies, or whatever else they might need. They can change circumstances and affect others around you or even your luck. So call on the angels to have luckier days. I am listing angels first because they are your first line of defense and protection against anything or anyone that wants to harm you. They can also help banish your fear and make you stronger so you won't be as impacted by any dark beings you come across.

How to know they are around: When angels are around, you might experience pressure changes which cause your ears to pop. You might also find feathers in unusual places. They also communicate through rainbows, unusual clouds and through music. When they are around, miraculous events happen and you feel love, warmth and positive energy. You might also get goosebumps and a positive, loving, warm sensation. You will also likely receive lot of signs through the world around you, including via things you see and hear, or animal messengers, among others.

Here is a bulleted list of signs or symptoms angels are around:

- Ringing ears
- Seeing rainbows
- Angel references in the world around you
- Finding feathers in unusual places
- Miraculous events
- Pressure changes in the air that make your ears pop
- Getting goosebumps
- Unexplained feeling or warmth or hot flashes and sensations
- A warm and loving sensation
- Feeling like you are getting an angel hug with wings
- Positive and encouraging signs from the universe around you

- Seeing wings or other angelic symbols in the world around you
- Receiving messages through music, overheard conversation or things you see
- Synchronicity

How to protect yourself: In this case, the angels are your key to protection against dark forces. Yes, they are sweet and loving, but they are also powerful warriors. You can think of them like your personal elite guard. Though demons may be powerful, there is nothing as powerful as the light. If you are smart, you'll want them in your life. Invite them into your life, and watch magical changes happen. Angels are of the light which means you need to invite them in, in order for them to work on your behalf. They will always guide us though, even when we are not asking them to. In chapter eleven, I address how to recognize and handle fallen angels.

Tips*:* If there is one angel to call on, it is Archangel Michael. He is the commander of armies of angels so he's well connected, and very powerful. Also, he is an excellent warrior and protector so he is perfect to call on for help with anything dark or if you are scared or need protection for any reason. The spiritual realm is a telepathic one so you can simply think (or say), "Archangel Michael, help me, protect me, and (fill in the blank)." Angels aren't limited by time and space the way we are, so they can help multiple people at the same time.

In addition to Archangel Michael, other angels of protection and clearing are Raphael, Chamuel, Jophiel, Azrael, Seraphiel, and Metatron.

It is important to ask for clearing and protection so that the angels have permission to assist. Doing this regularly can really help transform your life.

Types of Angels

There are many different kinds of angels that work with us. Most people are familiar with guardian angels. Guardian angels are assigned to us at or before birth and they know us intimately and are specifically tasked with giving support, assistance and guidance. You can think of a guardian angel as a guidance counselor, best friend and loving parent all rolled into one. They are there with us through thick and thin and they love us unconditionally. There are also archangels who work with guardian angels and other angels and help direct them on bigger projects. Each archangel has specific areas they focus on. So you can imagine an archangel who focuses on the environment has a whole host of angels that work with on that topic. An archangel that focuses on music will have a particular group of musical angels that they work with. For this reason, archangels are very powerful angels to call on because when you ask for their support, you are getting not just their assistance, but the assistance of all the angels they work with. Another wonderful type of angel to work with is a specialty angel. For every task, there is an angel in charge of it. So you may ask the angel in charge of that topic to help, even if you don't know their name. For example, if you need help with parking, you can ask the parking angels to assist you. If you are struggling with math, you can ask the math angels to help you and so on.

One important thing to keep in mind about angels is that they honor our free will. That means that they will be around and they will observe, but until we ask for their assistance, they will not intervene. This is an important point because unless we ask, they will give us guidance and energetic support but will not step in. They want to help us so when we don't ask, it's as if they are unemployed and nobody likes to be unemployed, especially angels. Some people are concerned about asking the angels for help too much but there is no such thing. The angels are an unending resource for support.

The key to changing your life in magical ways is asking for the angels help and doing so regularly. Because we have the right to change our mind, we must continually ask for help for the things we want to shift in our lives. By doing so, it's as if you are pushing the magic button. I highly recommend it.

How to Ask for Help

To ask for their help, you can simply mentally ask for their support and know that since the spiritual realm is telepathic, they will hear you. You can also say your prayers out loud or write them down for additional clarity and power. The clearer we are on what we are asking for, the more powerful the prayer is. Sometimes our thoughts can be jumbled and unclear, so if you are thinking your prayer, be sure to be clear. Ask the angels for help with whatever you would like assistance with specifically. You can ask for general help, but I also recommend asking for specific help. Think about what would happen if you went to a restaurant and just ordered food. Who knows what you might get! Asking for what you want in specific terms helps ensure that your order with the universe gets delivered correctly. In many ways, it really is as simple as, "Ask and ye shall receive." Most people just aren't asking and as soon as I started to ask, my life shifted in ways I could hardly believe possible.

The main reason I am writing about angels in this book is to convey how stellar they are at protecting people. If you ask, they can intervene directly on your behalf. They might also change the perception of those near you or provide assistance in another way entirely. Once I was walking in New Orleans and felt suddenly unsafe on my way to a voodoo store. It was dark and there was no one else out except for a few people a few blocks ahead of my friend and me. I asked the angels for protection and when we walked by they were looking up but they did not acknowledge us despite the fact that we walked a foot from where they were sitting on the sidewalk. I believe they did not see us which would have been nearly impossible as my friend and I were literally one foot away. I feel that the angels made us invisible to them to protect us. After we got away from them, the feeling of imminent danger went away. If you want more information on angels specifically, you can read one of my three books on the subject: *Angels: How to Understand, Recognize, and Receive Their Guidance; Angels and Manifesting;* or *Archangels and Ascended Masters.*

TWO
Ghosts

Other names: Spirits, apparition, shade, specter, spook

What are they? A ghost is simply a person (or animal or other incarnated form) whose body has died but whose spirit has stayed on the earth plane and not crossed into the light on the other side. This means that they have only the perspective from their most recent life and do not have the greater perspective and understanding they will receive when they cross into the light and remember other lives, soul mission and purpose, etc. Most ghosts are inherently sad, angry, or frustrated which is why they didn't cross to begin with. Being around a ghost is kind of like being around an upset, invisible person who is lost or confused. Some ghosts have awareness they are dead and others do not.

How to know they are around: If they are around, you may experience temperature changes, EVPs (electronic voice phenomena), mechanical and electrical malfunctions, objects moving around, a sense of being watched, apparitions, hearing noises or talking when no one is around in the space with you, etc.

How to protect yourself: Ask the angels to protect you and honor your boundaries. If a ghost is in your home, tell them they must leave or go into the light and then ask the angels to help them cross. If the ghost precedes you in the space, they may be stubborn about leaving (after all, they were there first). If the ghost tries to get in your body, tell them 'no' and ask the angels for clearing and protection. Ghosts will sometimes do this to have a physical experience or to manifest an addiction like drinking.

Where to find them: Ghosts will often hang out where they died though they can move to somewhere they liked in life or feel comfortable with in the present. They also are attracted to those who can sense them, have good energy, or who can help them cross (whether or not that person knows they can do this). So in many ways, a person can be haunted just as much as a place can. Some ghosts like to be relatively undisturbed and may stay where live people are not present, while others like to be around people. It really depends on the personality and preferences of the ghost. There are ghosts that know they are ghosts and those that don't. For those who are unaware, they may continue to live their end of life experiences over and over again. For example, many battle or war sites have never-ending ghost battles happening. When I went to Gettysburg, I experienced battles like this. There are many places in the south where the Civil War battles were so brutal that this still happens. While newer real estate developments may have less haunting experiences, it is not always the case. It is true that many new developments are built on native burial grounds and when this happens, the spirits often become restless.

Tips: Signs a ghost is around can include lights flickering, electrical problems, objects moving on their own, plumbing problems, unexplained noises, apparitions, or cold spots. If you are sensitive or psychic, you might also feel drained or sad around ghosts since most ghosts are not happy and sometimes draw energy from their live hosts. Sage can dispel any energies left behind by ghosts but is usually not enough to actually get them to leave or cross over.

Poltergeists

While it is possible for a ghost to learn how to manipulate matter, to get angry and move things around, I believe that most hauntings that are labelled as poltergeists may actually involve something that is not and has never been human. In many cases, I believe djinn are actually responsible for supposed poltergeist activity. I will discuss djinn in greater detail in chapter twelve. Djinn are known in the west as genies, probably made most famous by TV shows like *I Dream of Jeannie* or the movie *Aladdin*.

Ghost Stories

I have so many ghost stories, it's hard to know what to include here! If you want to read more on this topic specifically, I recommend reading my book *Diary of a Ghost Whisperer* which is filled with my experiences with earth bound spirits or ghosts.

Growing up, I was plagued by ghosts that tried to get into my body and terrorized my dreams. There was one particular ghost that was known to stand at the foot of my bed and watch me sleep. He tried to possess my body, just to have a physical experience, but also because he wanted to drink. Did you know that addiction doesn't have to end when the body dies? I have found that lots of ghosts like liquor and when people drink, their natural body defenses go down. It is for this reason that sometimes when people drink too much and black out or lose time, they are not always in charge. In fact, I think it's no coincidence that the old name for liquor is spirits. If you drink too much, spirits literally take over. As I got more sensitive and psychically aware, I at first minimized my drinking and then I stopped completely to have better protection. Even now, when I go to a bar or nightclub, if there is a lot of spirit activity and a lot of drinking, I may have to leave because it can get unpleasant for me.

Ghosts can haunt a particular place or they can move around much like we can. Ghosts will often do the same things we might do. Nevertheless, I was surprised one night when I went to a late night movie with a friend and glanced over to see a ghost watching the movie. It was particularly curious to me because the movie I was watching was *Insidious 2* which features depictions of ghosts, the other side, and psychics. He left me alone and I left him alone, but I thought it was so funny to see him there. Ghosts will sometimes show in the most unexpected places!

I came across another ghost in a place I didn't expect when I was doing a clearing in a ranch in Wyoming. I walked into the living room and there was an elk standing there, well the ghost of an elk anyway. Once I got over my surprise, I communicated with him psychically and got that he had apparently been killed by a long range with a rifle. He had not expected it and didn't know what to do so he stayed with what was left of his body (or, in this case, his head) and had been hanging out in that living room ever since he had been shot. I have never liked most mounted heads or animal skins and I think this is partially why; sometimes, there are tagalongs that come with them.

For whatever reason, I have come across several ghost cats and had one living with me for a while. He would jump on the bead and 'knead biscuits' on me and purr. It was quite sweet actually! Ghost dogs are not as common in my experience. Essentially anything with a body whose soul dies and the soul does not cross into the light can become a ghost. I have come across ghost vampires and werewolves, as well. In most cases, spirits become ghosts when they are confused and traumatized or are simply not ready to let go. If they are ready, I try to explain to them why it's a good idea to cross into the light and assist them to do so. When I do clearing work, in many ways I act like a ghost counselor. I explain to them that it's wonderful on the other side and that if they go over there and don't like it, they can simply come back (which they never do because it's so great on the other side). Often times, just like their live counterparts, ghosts just want someone to listen to them. Can you imagine being stuck in between and being upset and no one (aside from psychics) being able to hear you? That is why those who are psychic may be plagued with ghosts; we are the only ones who can hear and it can get lonely for the ghosts. Also, those that can see and sense spirits usually also have the ability to help them cross into the light (these abilities tend to go hand in hand). Unfortunately, getting training to do this type of work is not very typical, so for those that are gifted in this area, it can be very frightening when ghosts are frequently coming up to them. It took me many years to understand what was going on and get the training I needed so that I would not be scared of them when they appeared. If you sense ghosts, know that it is possible to get training and that you don't have to be afraid or feel out of control.

It may be helpful to remember that a ghost is simply a person without a body. There are nice people and not nice people and ghosts are the same. Some ghosts are sweet and others, malevolent. If you are dealing with a malevolent ghost, have strong boundaries and get help if you need to when dealing with the ghost. If the ghost is sweet, they may not present you any problems, though it really is best for all if they can cross over. A ghost can't really progress until they go into the light, do a life review, and move on. Asking the angels for help protecting you and assisting the ghost is always a good idea. Letting an angry or malevolent ghost hang out in your place is not a good idea as they bring a lot of dark and negative energy in your space. Keeping that kind of energy in your space for long periods of time can result in illness, problems in relationships, financial problems, major mechanical and plumbing problems, and accidents. It is, in my opinion, well worth the effort and expense to deal with these kinds of problems early on or you might end up with bigger problems on your hands down the road. Also, when there are ghosts around, it is highly likely that there are also dark entities or demons around too, particularly if the ghosts are malevolent and that is definitely not something you want in your home.

THREE
Demons and Dark Entities

Other names: Diablo, fiend, ghoul, hellion

What are they? Demons and dark entities are incarnated dark beings who feed on and create dark energies and emotions like pain, anger, frustration, sadness, fear, anxiety, depression, chaos, and disorder. They influence our thoughts and feeling and the circumstances around us to get what they want. These beings are on the energy plane and rarely show up physically though those who are very psychic may see them clairvoyantly.

How to know they are around: When they are influencing you, it may feel like you got up on the wrong side of the bed that morning. Things do not go well and, on the extreme end, you might experience accidents, unexplained pain, dissension, and technology and communication problems. You also will likely feel extra grouchy, sensitive or angry, depending on what your triggers are and the type of entity that is around. In the paragraphs below, I go into further detail on the types of entities and other signs that they are around.

I've included a bulleted list of dark entity and demon symptoms for easy reference for this category for you as well:

- Having a bad day, things going badly
- Accidents
- Being clumsy
- Unexplained pain or injuries
- Communication problems
- Dissension in relationships
- Illness
- Allergies
- Technology problems
- Stagnation or lack of flow
- Blocks to finances and opportunities
- Sadness or depression
- Feeling overwhelmed
- Panic attack
- Loud or overwhelming music or background noise
- Negative thoughts or feelings about yourself or others
- Hearing creepy or scary voices encouraging you to do bad things
- Feeling nauseous, lightheaded, and ungrounded
- Missed connections or opportunities

How to protect yourself: Asking the angels and specifically Archangel Michael to protect you, your thoughts, and your energy field is crucial. Since these beings often negatively influence technology or our environments, I recommend asking for protection for anything you use or rely on. As I got stronger and more connected, my electronics, vehicles or other tools became a target, so asking for an extension of protection on your belongings is extremely helpful as well. I'd like to note that since these beings are like supernatural parasites that feed on certain emotions and feelings, your thoughts and actions can either feed or starve them. If you starve them, they will eventually leave to find better food. If you feed them the energies such as fear, pain, anxiety, stress, doubt, depression, etc., they will continue to feed and attempt to perpetuate any cycle you are in that allows them to continue feeding. Actively working to clear them and any residues they leave behind is recommended in addition to working to shift any patterns or behaviors which create the kind of energy that attracts them. This is often a process which involves making many changes over a period of time. Much like illness, the doctor can give you antibiotics which will help you fight an infection in the short term, but unless you get stronger and healthier in the long-term, you will get sick again. It is important to not just clear the beings that are amplifying any problems but to heal whatever is in you that is attracting them as well. Whatever is happening in the energy plane is often a mirror of what is happening in the physical. If you are in a toxic job, in poor health, or have a negative mindset, all these things can provide a huge lure for these types of beings. Asking the angels to help you shift any unhealthy patterns is one of the most powerful prayers of all in terms of releasing any hold the darkness has over you.

Where to find them: Demons and dark entities can be anywhere, though they thrive in places where there is stagnation, chaos, disease, depression, poverty, or anything else that creates pain, sadness or hurt for people. Consequently, places where most people wouldn't probably want to hang out is where you will find them. They are also often found alongside ghosts because when a person dies, their attachments don't necessarily move on. If there are a lot of cockroaches, flies, or other pests about, it is almost a sure sign that dark entities are around.

Tips: It is important to ask for clearing and protection so that the angels have permission to assist. Doing this regularly can really help transform your life. Since we have free-will and can change our mind, it's important to keep asking every day or even a few times a day so the angels feel confident they have your permission to support and help. It's also important to look at what pattern or behavior may be attracting them and then shift that, so you are no longer providing the food (negative energies) that is appealing to these beings.

Stories About Entities

One of the signs of entities that I find to be a clear indicator is allergies. I used to have horrible allergies and struggled for years. I started the process of NAET™, Nambudripad's Allergy Elimination Technique, an allergy elimination treatment to eliminate my allergies after trying unsuccessfully to heal them through allergy shots. I was going through this process at the same time as I was learning about and expanding my psychic gifts. As I developed my gifts and got healthier, I began to notice a pattern that when I sensed demons and dark entities, I also had allergy attacks. Now I have no allergies unless someone around me has attachments or I am in a place where they are collected. It can be incredibly dramatic as I may be completely allergy free and then someone sits next to me with attachments and I suddenly feel a horrible allergy attack with itchy eyes, sneezing, and a foggy headed feeling. I was tempted to think that perhaps I was just allergic to the perfume they were wearing, but consistently, when I cleared their attachments that were attacking me, the allergies went away too. Then when I asked my angels and spirit guides to show me what was going on energetically, they showed me how a lot of attachments will literally be generating and spreading bacteria, viruses, and allergens in the air around them. This means that if you are near them, you can quickly get sick, or at the very least feel tired and run down as your immune system goes into overtime to try to handle the onslaught to its defenses.

If you are around entities consistently, you might be constantly sick, have recurrent allergies, and feel very low energy as your body is in stress mode and on alert from attacks to the immune system. I have had several jobs and periods of my life when I struggled with illness, allergies, and feeling run down all the time. I now understand how the entities that were around me contributed to this. Think of dark entities and demons as decay and illness, things we generally do not want in our lives. Know that they literally affect matter and generate nasty things to make us sick so they can feed on our stress, anxiety, lethargy, etc.

Another unusual symptom that I was surprised by, once I noticed the correlation, is distorted music or sounds which make it difficult to hear what you are trying to listen to, including those you might be speaking to, an important announcement, or even your own thoughts. There have been several situations in which I was speaking with a friend, talking about something significant and right at a crucial point of the conversation, the music would mysteriously get extremely loud. There is sometimes also what I call the "funhouse effect" where the sound would get distorted at the same time. For example, the rhythm on a recording might be off or sound like it's speeding up or slowing down. There might also be other things that create the noise like dogs barking, an airplane drowning out sound, sirens, or other loud noises. When this happens, ask the angels for help with communication and clearing anything that might be interfering. In locations where there are too many openings to the dark, you might need to actually leave the space in order to finish the conversation or hear whatever it is you were trying to hear.

Sirens or alarms of any kind may be a psychic warning. They can be a warning of something physical that is coming or about to happen or they could be a warning of something in the psychic or energy plane. Whenever I hear one, I ask for protection and insight on what the attack is about. If the siren or alarm is in your house like a smoke detector, you may be being notified that there is something in your home that is attacking or damaging.

Just like various animals look different and have unique diets, different entities have a distinct set of qualities and feed on various energies specific to them. One type of entity may feed on anxiety while another feeds on lethargy and depression. I've laid out some examples of common entities and what they feed on below. Know there is a lot of variety in this world, just as there are many different kinds of species in the physical world.

- Spiders – feed on and create fear
- Snakes – feed on and create pain
- Trilobite (a type of prehistoric marine animal that looks like a large insect often found in the fossil record) - feed on and create sadness and hopelessness

- Gremlins – feed on and create depression, malaise and isolation
- Flies – feed on and create dissension, miscommunication and hopelessness
- Moths – feed on and create dysfunctional sexual energy and being fooled or falling for illusion
- Cockroaches – feed on and create stagnation, clutter, filth and grime
- Tar babies – slimy entities that create stagnation, create plumbing problems and blockages in flow, physically and symbolically

If you struggle with the emotions or feelings associated with a particular entity, it is highly likely that you have entities of that type feeding on you. If you are releasing the type of food they feed on, they will be drawn to you. You can ask the angels to remove them and then work on shifting how you feel so that you don't attract more. This is not always a simple process but, with patience and diligence, you can clear dark entities and change your behavior and lifestyle so you are not attracting dark beings who magnify and then feed on any unpleasant feelings you have.

Dark Entities Are Very Commonplace

I get the question a lot, "Do I have anything on me?" And the answer to that most times is yes, though I think what people usually mean is "Do I have an Arch Demon attached?" (a very powerful type of demon) to which the answer is no. Most of us are dealing with learning to shift and release unhealthy patterns through experience. As a result of this, we tend to have beings feed on us as we are going through this learning process. Just like there are lots of helpful and malevolent bacteria, there are energy beings that harm and help working on and around us. There are helpful beings like angels and harmful beings like dark entities, but ultimately it's all about choice. I don't like to use the terms good and evil because often we have to try something dark in order to understand why it's not a good long term choice. When a child doesn't know any better and does something with negative consequences, the action is not evil, the child simply didn't know any better. It is the same in terms of life choices here. We must learn on our own, through experience, the consequence of various actions. This is why trying to save those who are consumed in darkness is often a losing battle. Until those souls have learned the consequences of their actions, they will not understand why certain actions might be better or worse for them and so are bound to repeat the pattern. It is good to help people but make sure those you are trying to help are ready to be helped. If we try to help and save those from dark forces who have not yet learned the consequences, we often retard their growth and suffer ourselves. In essence, we have a lose-lose situation instead of a win-win environment which is what the light principles operate in.

If you are in the pattern of always trying to rescue others, redirect the focus back to yourself and make sure you are helping others in way that empowers them to change rather than trying to fix things, and ask the angels to help you with any unhealthy patterns of over-helping. This is a big problem for many of us who have a life-purpose that involves helping; we often forget ourselves in the equation.

Levels of Influence

In my experience with demons and dark entities, there are three levels of influence and attack. The first is when they are around and subtly influencing. The second level is when they are attached to a person's energy body or energy field and influencing overtly. The third and most serious level is outright possession in which case the entity has taken full control of the body. Possession is real but highly unusual. The first two levels are very common.

With the first level, the person they are impacting will be influenced by suggestion or thoughts. The person may be confused and think that the suggestions or thoughts from the entities are their own. Only if they are very psychic are they likely to tell that these suggestions are coming from outside their own mind. The second level or attachment is also fairly common. In this level of influence, the dark entity or demon is directly attached to the person's energy field and, in some cases, their consciousness. If the entity is an energy feeder, then they may simply draw on energy from their host. There are many energy parasites, like snake entities, that simply clamp on and draw on the energy and pain they create. I had one client who came into me for knee pain and was confused when acupuncture made the pain worse. I was shown that the snake entity didn't like the needles and sort of chewed on her knee during and after acupuncture so this normally healing procedure was causing her more pain until the entity was removed. If the entity is more complex and intelligent, it can more directly influence thoughts and actions and, in some cases, even thought patterns. I have seen some highly intelligent entities that will attach to our brain and sort of rewire thoughts and neural patterns so that the outcomes are more in their favor. When they do this, it is always against our self-interest.

In outright possession, the being has taken full control of the hosts body and mind. Again, this is quite rare, but it does happen. It should be noted that in the Catholic Church, they list infestation, oppression, and obsession as pre-cursers to possession. When this occurs, the host will speak in a different voice or even language. There will clearly be someone else in the body who may exhibit supernatural strength. They will also experience convulsions, vomiting/and or gagging and other bodily reactions. It is also possible that they will levitate or do other things that are not generally humanly possible. There may also be intense anger or violence at religious objects or phrases. If this is happening to you or someone you know, I highly recommend getting assistance. A priest can do an exorcism or another trained professional may also be able to help, but this is not work for the faint of heart and should not be undertaken on a whim. When you are dealing with powerful dark beings like this, you must have incredibly strong boundaries yourself and be solidly in the light or you will likely be hurt or scarred in the process. I should note also that when possession like this happens, it is sometimes but not always because the person involved has been messing with or inviting dark energies and beings into their life. For this reason, I strongly caution against dabbling in the occult without getting an education first. Invocating dark beings you are unfamiliar with is a recipe for disaster. I also caution against using Ouija™ or other fortune telling boards without proper protection as they can open a door and you may not like the being who answers that door and steps into your life.

Our lives are very much like a garden; think of dark energy beings as weeds and flowers, fruits, and vegetables as the light. You must weed out the dark stuff you don't want because it will show up anyway, even when you don't plant it. The good stuff usually has to be planted and cultivated, so make sure you are inviting angels and other light beings into your life and saying no to the dark by weeding it out regularly. The good news is, the more consistently you weed out the dark stuff and don't allow it to take hold, the less you have to weed and the more you can enjoy the fruits of life.

FOUR
Faeries

Other names: Fairy, faery, the little people, the wee people, the wee folk, fey

What are they? Faeries are a type of highly magical creature that resides in a parallel plane to us on the earth but are known from time to time to pop over and intermingle with us here in the human world. Those with the sight (seeing things from the non-physical realm) may be blessed enough to see them, which is rare; they normally steer clear of us as we are thought of as dangerous and, at the very least, careless. Faeries are elemental beings, which means they are connected to each of the four elements: earth, air, wind, and fire. Just like witches or humans, for that matter, they can be light or dark. Elementals and faeries (which are a type of elemental) are connected to one particular element. There are earth faeries, water faeries, etc.

How to know they are around:

- Seeing sparkling or twinkling lights
- Hearing faerie music
- Mischievous pranks: a common one is switching shoes, switching shampoo for conditioner etc.
- Losing time
- Seeing faeries in nature or interacting with you
- Finding faerie rings

How to protect yourself: Generally speaking, if you don't mess with them, they don't mess with you; however, they can be mischievous with humans. They also don't take kindly to abuse of nature or the planet. If they witness you abusing Mother Nature, they may make some trouble for you. Like most beings, they can be light or dark and while we tend to think of faeries as playful and fun, there are those that are dark and malevolent. If you find yourself being attacked or opposed by some dark faeries, ask the angels for protection and to clear any magic they may have cast on you.

Tips: There are some very playful faeries that are lovely to have around. You can make your home or garden more welcome to them by leaving them offerings of candy, jewelry, or shiny objects. They love flowers and gardens of a less ordered and more wild variety. They love to party and have fun and, if you are lucky, you might observe them having a faery party. It is rare for a human to see them, but those that do have been known to have so much fun, they get enchanted with the experience and never come back to the human world.

Where to find them: They reside in the faerie plane which is one of the planes adjacent to the human plane. That said, they can come into our plane or traverse between the planes. They also have the magic to bring humans to their plane though this is a very rare experience. They will show themselves to humans they trust and like or sometimes those they strongly dislike as well. They can also be found in nature. Faeries that are of the earth element may dwell in caves or forests while water elementals love the ocean, streams and ponds. Air elementals are in the air around us and in the atmosphere. Fire elementals may be found in lightning storms or anywhere that you might find extreme heat or fire, like a volcano or deep in the earth.

The faeries are guardians of the natural realm and often get frustrated with humans for being careless and destructive. If you are a good steward of the environment, the faeries will like you. If you are careless and destructive, the faeries will disapprove and may play tricks on you.

Faerie Time

Since faeries are ultra terrestrial and simply from another plane or dimension, time does not move at the same pace on their plane as it does on ours. It is reported that those who are transported to their plane may feel they have been gone for minutes or hours, but years may have passed in the human plane.

Types of Faeries or Beings from the Faerie Plane

- Pixies
- Sprites
- Flower faeries
- Leprechauns (not faeries but of the same plane)

- Gnomes
- Selkies
- Devas
- Elves
- Brownies
- Tuathe de Danann
- Merpeople
- Nymphs
- Salamanders
- Sylphs
- Undines

There are water faeries like water sprites, water nymphs, and merpeople (beings with the head and torso of a man and the body of a fish) and earth faeries such as flower faeries, brownies, etc. Sylphs are air elementals and Salamanders are fire elementals.

Connecting with Faeries

If you want to connect with the faeries, you can do several things to increase the odds of them showing themselves to you.

- Be a good steward of the environment
- Be kind to faeries
- Leave them gifts and use faerie friendly plants
- Invite them in
- Be open to them
- Look for them at twilight or night time when they are more visible
- Have faerie houses and create faerie gardens

Gifts for the Faeries

If you want to leave gifts for the faeries, here are a few things they love! You can leave the following things outside with the intention that they are for them:

- Coffee
- Shiny objects and jewels
- Sweet treats
- Orderliness (they do not like messy homes)
- Happy, fun music
- Low light environments
- Faerie houses

Faerie Gardens

Planting a faerie garden can be a great way to connect with faeries and create an inviting ambiance for them. Here are just a few of the plants and trees that they like, though there are many more.

- Ash
- French lavender
- Oak
- Rosemary
- Shasta daisy
- Thyme
- Toadstools
- Verbena
- Vervain
- Willow
- Zinnias

Confusion between Djinn and Faeries

I feel it is important to note that there often seems to be a lot of confusion between the faeries and the djinn (djinn are more commonly known as genies in Western terminology). Both are extra dimensional or ultra-terrestrial and have magical qualities. They both interact with humans, and both can be light or dark. That said, they come from different realms and planes and are different types of beings altogether. In my experience, while the faeries can come into our plane, they are a lot more hesitant to interact with humans on a regular basis unless they have established trust. The djinn, on the other hand, will more often connect with humans and interact with us physically as they are shape shifters. I believe that this is partially due to the fact the djinn were banished from our plane whereas the faeries left voluntarily to escape human intrusion and attack. More on that in the chapter on Djinn.

Messages from the Faeries

Recently while meditating, I received messages from the faeries, so I thought I would pass them on. The message was different from each type of elemental. Here they are:

Air elementals: We are here helping you clear the air you breath. We ask that you plant more trees and stop burning fossil fuels. You have the technology to use clean energy. There are those who are stifling this right now. Ask us to help. We also encourage you to be light in spirit. You are free to explore and be light and play. Ask for our help and remember to breath. So much would be resolved if you all breathed deeply. Breathing deeply helps you think more clearly. Breathe and believe in magic for we are real.

Fire elementals: Remember your passions and honor us who stoke the fires and keep light alive. We work in your technology and, without fire, humanity would be literally in the dark. Remember what we offer and how we can help. Ask us for help with passion, light and inspiration. We are here for you but remember also the potential destructive aspect of fire. Too many of you are burning yourself away with stress. Remember too that balance is the key for those in the earth plane. Too little fire and you wither and die from lack of passion, too much and you burn yourselves out. We can help you find your passions and keep them alive without getting burned. Call on us for help and remember to respect fires' power.

Earth elementals: We are here to take care of the plants and the animals and the earth itself. Too often you disregard this world or try to conquer it. It all works so much better when we can work together, many humans are still learning this lesson. We also are helping your crops and trying to stop environmental pollution and destruction. Remember, the earth is not your enemy. We are here to help, call on us to help with these things. The time is coming when our realms will be closer and closer as they were once united. Do not destroy the earth before this happens.

Water elementals: Water is life, and without water, there is no life. We help sustain the very thing that allows for life to exist. We help the flow of life through the earth and plants and animals. There are many problems with water as humans are both greedy for it and are not appreciative of it. The way that water is being used is not sustainable. We are trying to help humanity and the earth learn how to use this precious resource lovingly. Ask for our help and know that water is alive. Treat it with respect as you would a plant or an animal. Love it and it will love you back. Disregard it and abuse it and it will leave. This is what is happening with many of the droughted places in the world. Humanity needs to love and appreciate water again for it to return.

Faerie Stories

As I was starting my psychic practice, I started to see faeries and it was so magical. They often showed up for me at night when I was in the in-between sleep and awake state. That is when we can most easily connect with their realm. The most common type that I would see literally looked like Tinkerbell! I would see a little ball of light with a small figure inside. They were of different colors, sometimes green or red and they always felt very fun and playful.

I also had a faerie queen show up in my bedroom. I awoke to her looking at me as she floated from the corner of my room. She was very supportive and loving and sharing her presence with me. She did not say anything, but I knew it was significant and that it was a blessing she was there. She was beautifully dressed in various shades of lavender and purple, had red hair and a crown. She had beautiful wings and even though she was floating, her wings were not moving, she was just magically floating there. I knew from her presence that I was supported. Ever since then, I have understood my connection with their realm and known that the faeries were helping me.

A couple of years after that happened, the first ever *Festival of Faerie* was held in Lafayette, Colorado, my hometown and I helped them by doing some pro-bono PR and media and communications work. There are many, many faeries in Lafayette so it is not surprising that this festival is held there and that it was while I was living there that I ended up connecting with this realm.

If you want to connect with faeries, just let them know you would like to do so. Like the angels, they can hear our thoughts.

They are most friendly to those who help them with their work, are supportive and friendly, are good stewards of the environment, and believe in faeries, of course.

FIVE
Dragons

Other names: Dracon, draco, drake, drakon

What are they? Dragons have a very strong reputation in our world and stereotypically we tend to think of them as large scaly creatures that live in a mountain, breathe fire and love gold, just like in *The Hobbit*. This is just one of the many types of dragons and, like faeries, they are associated with one of the elements. A water dragon is going to be very different than an earth-based dragon. The word dragon comes from the word drakon and means the seeing one. While it may be tempting to associate dragons with dinosaurs, they are very different creatures. Dragons are much more intelligent and closer to mammals than dinosaurs.

How to know they are around: If dragons are around, you may be getting a lot of references to dragons and feel their strong and powerful energy. You might also notice power surges and electrical energy. If you are very psychic, you may also sense them with your clair-senses such as clairvoyance and clairaudience. It is possible to have dragons as spirit guides. If a dragon is serving as your spirit guide, they are a powerful ally for manifestation.

How to protect yourself: You are highly unlikely to come into contact with a dragon. In the event that you do, do not try to take anything that belongs to them. Bad things will happen.

Where to find them: The stereotype is that they live in caves and land-based dragons are very much likely to. Their home environment depends on their element.

Tips: Dragons can have a lot of pride so it is inadvisable to insult them or push their temper. Even dragons that are of the light can be quick to anger. Dragons are very wise and have very powerful magic.

Types of Dragons

In mythology, there are many ways to categorize different types of dragons. There are European or Asian dragons, flying versus non-flying, fire-breathing versus non-fire-breathing, etc. There are even reportedly three-toed, four-toed, and five-toed dragons! Like many species, there can be a large variety of differences from one type to another. Because dragons are elemental creatures, a water dragon may look very different than the stereotypical earth-based dragon. And while there are those who claim to have seen them in physical form, for me they have remained in the energy plane alone.

However, just because a type of being is not in our plane does not make them any less real or important. Any time there are beings described in multiple cultures and mythologies all over the world, I think we have to consider that there is a reason they are so universally discussed.

Sometimes Equated with the Devil

Around the time that Christianity was taking hold, the dragon started to be equated with the devil or demons. Prior to Christianity, the mythology of dragons described some dragons as nice and some as not so nice. There are many depictions of Archangel Michael slaying the devil who is represented as dragon in form. The Bible even describes a dragon-like creature (Leviathan) in the book of Job, a part of the Old Testament. Here is an excerpt of that text:

> "I will not fail to speak of Leviathan's limbs, its strength and its graceful form. Who can strip off its outer coat? Who can penetrate its double coat of armor? Who dares open the doors of its mouth, ringed about with fearsome teeth? Its back has rows of shields tightly sealed together; each is so close to the next that no air can pass between. They are joined fast to one another; they cling together and cannot be parted. Its snorting throws out flashes of light; its eyes are like the rays of dawn. Flames stream from its mouth; sparks of fire shoot out. Smoke pours from its nostrils as from a boiling pot over burning reeds. Its breath sets coals ablaze, and flames dart from its mouth" (NIV).

In addition to the depictions of Saint Michael slaying the dragon or devil, there is also the story of Saint George who is listed as slaying a dragon. After the dragon is slain, the nearby townspeople convert to Christianity. While this can be taken as an allegory, the belief in many supernatural creatures did decrease with the growth of Christianity. I believe that Christianity simplified many beings previously thought of as a variety of non-human creatures and labelled them as devils, demons, or Satan.

While there may be some similarities to serpentine devils, dragons have a very different energy than devils and like humans and other incarnated beings, have free will and can therefore be either light or dark. They also have some similarities with dinosaurs in terms of their appearance but the similarities are very shallow indeed as dragons are smart and sophisticated magical beings that differ very much from cold-blooded, prehistoric and earth-based dinosaurs. I feel that dragons should be respected and treated with dignity for they are wise, intelligent, and sophisticated creatures.

Shanghai Dragon Pillar

I lived in Shanghai in 2010 and though I was not working as a psychic yet, I was really opening up to my gifts, taking psychic development classes and seeing the world very differently than I had just a couple of years before. While living in Shanghai, I heard an amazing story about a dragon there. Sometimes there are people, objects or places that are sort of psychically highlighted for me. That is the best way I can describe it, sometimes something looks brighter and catches my attention. When this happens, I don't know why, but I do know that there is a reason for it and that I should pay attention. This phenomenon was still relatively new to me as I had only recently opened up to my psychic gifts.

Shanghai is a huge metropolitan city and it has many large highways that run through it. There are many elevated highways with large support pillars beneath them. Most of these are plain and utilitarian with only bare concrete showing on the exterior. One in particular is decorated in silver-colored plating with gold dragons encircling the pillar. This particular pillar caught my eye and was psychically highlighted. I kept noticing it and wondering about it. For months I simply noticed it was different and wondered what the story was and then several months later, a story about the pillar appeared in one of the expat magazines and the mystery was explained. The pillars support the meeting of the Chengdu elevated highway and the Yan'an elevated highway. The story goes that in the 1990s, when they were constructing these supports, the construction crews had difficulty putting one particular support pillar in place and there was also a series of accidents at the site. Since the others went through without a problem, this was a mystery. After a lot of frustration and confusion about the situation, a monk was brought in to help understand what was going on. The monk meditated and reported that there was a dragon underneath the pillar that was not allowing the pillar to be put into the ground. The monk relayed that if they performed a series of rites there and decorated the pillar with dragons in the dragon's honor, that the dragon would allow for the pillar to be buried. In some versions of the story the monk also relayed that he had told too much and would not live long. The construction workers followed the advice and did the rites, decorated the pillar and then were able to lower it into the ground. It is said that the monk died seven days after the project was completed.

    There are those who say this is just a story and that the pillar was decorated simply because it was large and featured, but nevertheless, I find it interesting that this is the only pillar decorated in this way. Whether this story has any truth, there is strong fascination with dragons all over the world.

While I have never encountered a physical dragon, I have experienced quite a few of them in the energy plane. There are many dragons in the faerie plane and I have encountered dragon spirit guides before. They are very wise, very intelligent and very ancient. They live much, much longer than humans, they can live hundreds or even thousands of years. They are also very magical creatures and it is true that they do like treasure and valuable things such as magical objects. If you want someone to guard treasure, there is probably no better candidate than a dragon.

SIX
Vampires

Other names: The undead, Nosferatu (a type of vampire)

What are they? Vampires are supernatural creatures that feed on blood or life-force energy. We use the term vampire pretty openly now and people who are energy takers are even described as energy vampires. That said, there is a type of real supernatural vampire out there. There are also humans that crave and sometimes drink blood or fetishize it. You are probably more likely to run into the latter; however, there are real supernatural vampires out there who have abilities that humans definitely do not. Supernatural vampires can eat food and blend in with human society but without blood or life force energy, they will weaken and die. Of the supernatural type of vampire, there are those that are born and those who are turned or made. Yes, it is possible to be born a vampire, to vampire parents.

You can also be turned by a vampire and turned ones are the ones that most of our mythos comes from. Vampires that are born as vampires are more likely to have been born in a plane adjacent to ours. When this happens, they are extra dimensional and may be able to go back and forth between their plane and ours. If they are turned vampires, they may not even know about or be able to go to this other plane. Vampires that are turned do have abilities, but they may not have the full range of abilities of a born vampire. It is also possible for a born vampire to be born into the human plane, though this is rarer. There are a very small number of vampires in the human plane though the veils between their world and our world appear to be thinning.

Vampires have many magical abilities including their ability to glamour (compel, or hypnotize) people to get them to do their will. They can also wipe or erase memories. Consequently, it is possible that you have seen vampires or even been fed on and not remember it. They also can manipulate and control small animals and I believe this is why we often associate them with bats. There are nice vampires and those that are definitely not nice, just like humans. When a vampire feeds with permission, the experience can be magical and wonderful for both. When the vampire feeds without permission, it is violating and damaging even if the human survives. It is like the difference between making love and rape. The act is similar in terms of physical mechanics, but the results are completely different. I believe this is why vampires are both feared and romanticized; both scenarios exist and have happened to many. It is clear to me that many who are incarnated now have been vampires, have hunted vampires, and have been hunted by vampires. So vampires elicit strong feelings in many people, whether or not one has had real life experiences with them.

Vampires are very passionate and sensitive people. Some may find it surprising that I use the term people to describe vampires but they are people, just not human people. Vampires are very psychic and, yes, they are nocturnal, though they do not burst into flames from being in the sun but rather are weakened by it. Because of their magical abilities, they can manifest very powerfully and are good at turning circumstances in their favor. They can change the appearance of their age and do live longer and look younger than their human cohorts. They have magnetism and will draw people in even when they are not trying to.

How to know they are around: Vampires have a very specific energy; their energy field is very strong and intense and depending on whether they have lighter or darker tendencies, you may be drawn to them or feel fearful. Since they can magnetize you, you may feel drawn to them even when you don't feel like you should. Vampires, like faeries, can reside on their own plane or in our plane. The planes are adjacent to each other and they can also be in between planes so that you might hear them in our plane but not see them, for example. They can make themselves invisible while still interacting with physical matter. You might feel watched but can't see anyone. It is possible for them to speak human languages, but they also have their own language which is only partially audible to the human ear. If you hear them speaking in this language, it is often mistaken for birds or bat sounds but they do not actually sound like either. Once you have heard their language, you can differentiate it from birds or bats. They are fairly nocturnal, so you are more likely to hear them at night versus during the day. If you are very clairvoyant, you may be able to see that vampires have an orb. This orb is what allows them to do much of the magic that they do and is the center of their life force.

It is this orb that is targeted and damaged when vampires are staked in the heart. Hunter weapons are designed to destroy the orb specifically.

They often have beautiful and intense eyes. Their eyes may change color depending on whether they are thirsty, angry, or aroused, etc. You may feel drawn in to them in general, even from across the room. They are prone to moodiness and are, in my experience, more emotional than humans and very sensitive to the non-physical realm. And, of course, they crave and in fact need blood to survive. In regards to turned vampires versus born, the turned will have many of the same characteristics that born vampires do, but there are some limitations to what they will be able to do. I have also experienced that many turned vampires do not even know that there are vampires out there who have always been that way and were never human.

They are also extremely good at magic and manifesting and can move much faster than humans. They are also physically stronger and very smart. If you were to try to fight a vampire, you would probably come out on the losing end of the battle for many reasons such as their superior strength, speed, and many psychic abilities. Most vampires from the vampire plane also have extensive training in combat.

There are many types of vampires and while all are impacted by sunlight, most that I have encountered are simply weakened by it but not killed by it. The sun essentially drains them energetically and they, like humans, will get a sunburn, but it's the energy aspect that is the most damaging. Left too long in the sun, they will get incredibly depleted which is why they tend to spend most of their time out at night. I have heard of vampires that can die from sun exposure but I have never come across any of that kind personally. Vampires can also fly and when they do, they can move incredibly fast. You can see why they can be quite formidable. Vampires also look much younger than their age. How long they can live varies a lot, some can live just slightly longer than most humans (say one hundred or just over one hundred years old) while others may live to be thousands of years old. Many vampires living in the human realm look very young for their age. It is also possible for vampires to shift their age in any direction. Basically they can appear much older or younger than they are and then shift to appearing older very quickly. It is possible for a vampire toddler to appear as an adult. This makes their life very interesting as they have the intelligence of an adult but still are very young in terms of experience. Basically with a vampire, you can never really know how old they are.

Here is a bulleted list of signs or symptoms they are around:

- Seeing humans who are magnetic, young for their age, and have intense eyes that change color
- Losing time (your memories have been erased)
- Feeling faint or dizzy from blood loss
- Hearing unusual bird-like sounds at night
- Hearing sounds on the roof (when they fly they will often arrive on a roof)
- Feeling manipulated or doing things you wouldn't normally do and you don't know why

How to protect yourself: They can come in whether you invite them in or not. They can get in more easily actually than most since they can manipulate physical matter and walk through walls, etc. But they are very unlikely to try and come in unless you have a connection with them. If this is a concern of yours, asking the angels to help protect you is always a good idea. Follow your intuition, if you have a bad feeling about a place or a person and you suspect that they may be a vampire, I suggest leaving and asking the angels to guard you on your way out. There are vampire bars and nightclubs and if you go to one of their hangouts, you are more likely to run into them.

I feel it important to note that the boundaries you have with humans very much impact your boundaries with the non-human as well. By this I mean that if you have unhealthy boundaries with humans, you will also be especially vulnerable to supernatural creatures. This is because our choices and actions act as a message to the universe that says, "yes please, send more to me like this." So if you have poor boundaries with your boss, your spouse, your children, etc., you are sending a message to the universe that you want to be treated that way and you will get others sent to you that are more than happy to oblige by taking advantage of you. Enforcing healthy boundaries with humans ensures you are more protected with the supernatural as well.

Tips: While they can influence you without eye contact, it is easier for them to glamour you with direct eye contact. If you suspect someone is a vampire and you don't trust them, avoid eye contact. Do not assume that they are all bad; there are nice, friendly vampires as well.

Myths: Vampires are not, in fact, hurt by garlic or crucifixes. They can be somewhat weakened by water, but not to the extent that it will burn them. It is kind of like sunlight in that way, they would probably not opt to spend a lot of time in a swimming pool though they do bathe. They can use magic and some herbs, however, to protect themselves from the draining aspects of water. They also tend to not spend a lot of time in direct sunlight since it weakens them.

Vampire History

One of the reasons that vampires have so many of the powers they do is that they are descendants of the Nephilim. If you are unfamiliar with the Nephilim, they are the descendants of angels and man. They are described in the *Book of Enoch*, an apocryphal (not part of the recognized text) of the Catholic Church. When angels came and mated with humans, they had children. Their children had many different characteristics and some of them were more human in appearance than others. The vampires descended from a particular line of Nephilim and so many of their abilities, like their ability to manipulate physical matter and their ability to fly, come from their angelic lineage. Even their language is very close to angelic language. It is sad to me that many vampires assume they are evil (as society has told them they are), when they literally are descendants of angels. Some of the angels that mated with humans were fallen angels (motivated by the dark), but many of them were not fallen and were motivated by love. Even those descended from fallen ones are not necessarily dark. A child may be very pure in spirit even when the parent was not. Though vampires, in particular, bring up a lot of fear for most people, I'd like to share the idea that vampires are simply a different kind of person. Just as there are dark human and light humans (saints and serial killers, for example), so too there are dark vampires and light ones as well.

Vampire Pregnancy

Vampire pregnancies and human pregnancies are similar but there are differences. It is possible to become pregnant as a human from a vampire and never know you are pregnant. This sounds strange I realize, but with a vampire pregnancy, the mother does not show until immediately before she is to give birth. The mother might even continue to get her period but the pregnancy is happening energetically. The baby can be felt and may make noise. Many symptoms are similar to human pregnancy, moodiness, hormone swings, breast tenderness, feeling a child kick, etc. The main differences are the pregnancy will be energetic until suddenly right before birth, the mother will suddenly look physically pregnant. There is magic involved and immediately after the birth of the child, the mother's body returns to pre-pregnancy state. Like werewolf pregnancies, the pregnancy term is variable and I have heard of them lasting anywhere from one month to 9 or 10 months, each child and pregnancy is different even with the same parents. I am mentioning this in this section because it is not uncommon for human women to become pregnant with a vampire child and never know that they are pregnant. After the birth, the mother's memory is erased so that she has no memory of the birth or the child and the child is taken away.

Vampire Stories

I once did a reading for a client who described to me that she had moved to a neighborhood that was unusually quiet. She stated that there were almost no animals and at night it was too quiet except for the fact that she could hear birds that were not birds. I knew immediately that she had moved into a neighborhood in which a group of vampires resided. Though vampires, as a rule, do prefer human blood, they may hunt animals. Also, animals will also likely sense them and move away as they are a natural predator. In this case, I got that there was no danger to her or her family but she could tell that something was different and off from a normal human neighborhood.

Hollywood Connection

It has been revealed to me that there are many vampires in Hollywood and they are on a mission to help humans be less fearful of them. If you have paid attention recently, there have been many movies and television shows that have portrayed them in a sympathetic light or, at the very least, portrayed them as being human-like in their ability to have flaws, feel emotions, and be light, dark, or somewhere in the middle. Some recent examples are: *The Vampire Diaries*, *Vampire Academy,* and *Hotel Transylvania,* to name a few. We are being asked not to assume that someone is light or dark based on their form.

SEVEN
Werewolves

Other names: Loup-garou, lycan, lycanthrope, wolf-man

What are they? Werewolves are, in my opinion, not accurately named as these beings who have a human form can also transform into another form, but it is not a wolf exactly. Portrayals of werewolves in media that show them looking exactly like real-life wolves annoy me because that isn't what they look like at all, in my experience. In addition to werewolves, there are other werecreatures such as wererats, werecats, etc. If you are living a fairly typical life, you are not very likely to interact with shapeshifters. There are many kinds of shape-shifters. Even the werewolf is a type of shifter with two forms. There are shapeshifters that can shift into virtually any form. If you come into contact with a shifter, you are not likely to ever find out. Like vampires, they can be born or turned (made) as well. In my experience, there is interaction between vampires and werewolves and while they don't tend to like each other, there are also some that are mixed vampire and werewolf, much like what is depicted in the *Underworld* movie. As they say, truth is stranger than fiction, and I have witnessed it first-hand.

How to know they are around: If they are in animal form, you will most likely be aware of them from the sounds they make. They sound supernatural and do not sound like dogs or wolves, though some may dismiss their cries as being made by one or the other. If they are in human form, you are unlikely to recognize them as being different from humans, though they are known for their keen sense of smell and they do like raw meat.

How to protect yourself: Don't mess with a werewolf and they are likely not mess with you either. There are some werewolves who attack humans and others that stick to attacking animals. Avoid walking alone at night by yourself and if you are alone at night, ask for angelic protection.

Where to find them: Werewolves can be found anywhere that humans are though they like to be near places where they can hunt and transform. They tend to be pack creatures, so if you find one, you will likely be around others, though there are occasionally lone wolves.

Tips: They can transform at will and the full moon does not cause the transformation. That said, werewolves may feel more wild on the full moon though humans likely will too. As with vampires, there are nice werewolves and not nice werewolves. Some will treat humans well and some will disregard them or think of them much like animals. Don't make any assumptions either way with them. They are much stronger and faster than humans even when they are not in animal form, so if you have an altercation with a werecreature, be prepared for their inhuman strength, senses and reflexes. As with any type of potentially dangerous situation, ask the angels for help if you encounter one and are afraid.

Myths: While werewolves may be more inclined to turn on the full, moon, they are not compelled to. They are not immortal, though they are stronger and faster than their human counterparts.

Shapeshifters

While there are many different types of shapeshifters, werewolves and other were-creatures can only shift between their human form and their animal form. Other types of shifters such as the djinn can appear in many different forms.

Werewolf History

The idea of werewolves or humans that transform into wolves goes back to ancient Greek and Roman mythology. Ovid and Virgil both wrote about humans that transformed into wolves. The idea gained popularity in Europe during the 14th century. There are wolf-men described in Germanic, Viking, English, and French stories and traditions. In France, there were a series of attacks and cases which many attributed to werewolves. Later, during the witch trials, being a werewolf was sometimes one of the accusations. In Asia, the legends of weretigers or wereleopards were more common than the werewolf, which is more popular in Europe.

Stories About Werewolves

There are several times I have sensed and seen werewolves. If you are sensitive, you may sense them from their strong energy and a sort of wild and intense quality. I stayed in Mexico for about three months earlier this year and spent a good part of that time in Mexico City. There was a werewolf that lived in my neighborhood in Zona Rosa. Every night, between midnight and 2 am, he would howl. I felt he was a lone wolf and I think he was just honoring his need to howl. Most people would just dismiss the howl as being from a dog or perhaps a coyote or wolf in the nearby wilderness, but a werewolf howl sounds unique. As a psychic, I am constantly amazed at how often people dismiss things that are definitely paranormal because they either aren't paying attention, or they are not open minded enough to consider what is really going on.

Hollywood Portrayals

Just as with vampires, I believe there are werewolves in Hollywood who are helping to get humans more comfortable with the idea of having them in their midst. There are many television shows and movies lately, such as *The Twilight Saga* and *Teen Wolf*, which have portrayed them in a sympathetic light. It seems that the public is ready and willing to be open themselves to werewolves, at least in a fictional context. One newly popular genre is paranormal fiction, featuring werewolves and werebears. So, in theory at least, a certain segment of the population is more than willing to share the world with this particular type of supernatural creature.

Werewolf Stories

While I have seen werewolves out in public and recognized them by their energy fields, I have not had a lot of direct contact. There are those who have, however. One of the most striking stories of a werewolf or wolf-like man was in Elkhorn, Wisconsin. A series of residents reported seeing and, in some cases, being chased by a large dog or wolf-like creature. What is striking about these stories is that the stories described a similar creature and those who saw the being did not have connections with each other. After the series of sightings was reported, the being was not heard from again there.

EIGHT
Hunters

Other names: Slayers, kresniks

What are they? Hunters are those who hunt vampires, werewolves and other creatures. While this may sound like an episode of the television show *Supernatural*, hunters are real and do seek to kill and, in some cases, eradicate these groups entirely. Some hunters are purely human while others have a bit of magic and non-human elements as well.

How to know they are around: Most humans are not likely to pick-up on the presence of hunters though psychics or those who are very sensitive can. Psychics may not recognize what a hunter is if they come across one, however they may recognize that their energies are different than most humans. Hunters very typically have very spikey energy fields and most of them are caught up in aggressive and violent behavior so their energy can feel very dark. They are very psychic themselves which is how they identify vampires and other beings. They may be psychically gifted; they may also be able to psychically probe or retrieve information from others with psychic gifts. They do have weapons designed to kill or harm vampires, werewolves and other types of beings and may chase them in cars or on foot. Most hunters come from families of hunters, though new hunters may be adopted into their groups. The new hunters are unlikely to have any of the genetic traits that are inherited, like the spikey energy field or psychic abilities. One of the abilities that hunters have is to sense other supernatural creatures or to be able to see them for what they are, even when they appear to be in human form. If you are very clairvoyant, you may be able to see that they have what is called a cuspis. The cuspis is comparable to the orb for a vampire, but on a hunter it is based at the throat and is small and spikey.

How to protect yourself: If you are human, you are unlikely to need to protect yourself from them. If you are not human or have non-human friends, then they may be a threat. The first thing I recommend, to protect you from any threat, is to call on the angels, especially Archangel Michael, to protect you and remove danger. The second is to get yourself out of immediate danger which can often mean fleeing the place where the hunters are. Unfortunately, in my experience, a conflict between hunters and those they are hunting rarely ends without bloodshed, so unless you are willing to kill or be killed, disengagement is probably necessary. My hope is that as more people get educated on supernatural creatures, the desire to kill something just because it is supernatural or different will diminish. Yes, there are supernatural creatures that are dangerous, but killing supernatural creatures indiscriminately is not right either and simply escalates violence and malevolence between species.

Where to find them: Hunters are living in human society. Though they band together and work together, there are some areas where there are larger populations of them. There are a lot of hunters in Colorado, California, and also in Washington, DC. Not surprisingly, any place where there are a lot of supernatural creatures, you will also find a lot of hunters. Large cities will often have large supernatural populations and one reason is that it is easier for them to hide in large populations. There is one entire city in New Mexico which is only comprised of hunters. Anyone who is not a hunter would be an outsider. If you are psychic, you might detect them by their spikey energy field but aside from that, you are unlikely to know you are in their vicinity unless you are around supernatural beings who are being hunted or pursued by them.

Tips: If you encounter people you believe are hunters, I do not recommend engaging them. As a general rule, they take their work very seriously and do not tend to be open to outsiders knowing about them.

I was actually given the information from my spirit guide that the origin of hunters is similar to the origin of vampires and werewolves. Close to the beginning of humanity, angels came and mated with humans. Typical partnerships involved a male angel and a human woman. The descendants of these unions were called Nephilim. While some of these children had a lot of darkness, others did not. Not all who mated with human women did it against the will of God. Also, the child of a person who has bad intentions is not necessarily dark either. It is not fair for us to blame a child for the sins of their father. Nevertheless, some of them were dark and destructive and gave all Nephilim a bad name. Many Nephilim were killed in some cases because they were dark and dangerous and in other cases simply because they exhibited inhuman traits which frightened humans. Then came the flood which was to rid the world of the Nephilim but it was not successful and many survived. In fact, many of their descendants are here today. Some of them are passing as human while others are not in human society but are still living here on earth.

Some of the Nephilim more closely resembled humans while others had unusual traits and abilities. Bear in mind that not all angels look human in form. Some of them have, in addition to wings, animal features and don't resemble humans at all in their natural form though they can shift and create matter to appear however they please. When these angels had offspring with humans, some had features that made them noticeably different, while others did not. I was shown psychically that hunters actually descended from the Nephilim just like vampires, werewolves, and others, however those that later became hunters appeared more human. In essence, the hunters and vampires or werewolves descended very much from an Able and Cain situation in which one brother attacked the other and a rift was created. It is important not to place blame here, but to understand that though the hunters have been hunting supernatural creatures for millennia, they are direct descendants from the same Nephilim family tree. The feud goes back on both sides and the killing has been going on for so long, that no one remembers why. All that is known is hate and intolerance. It is my hope that as knowledge of these groups spread, there can be less hate and violence and more tolerance.

Most humans are not likely to come across hunters unless they are associating with other supernatural creatures. It should be noted that even within human history, there have been demographic groups who have been treated inhumanely because they were considered "other" and different or inferior. It is important to remember that just because someone or something is different, does not mean they are not valid. Just because someone is different, does not justify murder or persecution. Also, we should not judge one for the sins of another. If we were to judge the fate of humanity based on the actions of Adolf Hitler or Pol Pot, then humanity would be doomed. Thankfully, we have free will and there are also wonderful humans who are loving and positive. I feel we should have the same approach with non-human beings. Just because there are some vampires who kill and are cruel, that does not mean all vampires are that way. Let's not be judge, jury, and executioner for a type of being simply because some of those beings are dark. It is still smart to be safe and I also want hunters out there to know that I understand why they do what they do. In many cases there has been a need for protection from some and it is important to acknowledge that. Nevertheless, I think it's critical to assess, in each case, whether that particular being is dangerous and causing harm or whether you are condemning an entire race for the actions of a few.

NINE
Witches

Other names: Wizard, sorcerer/sorceress

What are they? Witches are individuals who practice witchcraft. Some think of witches as wiccans, but there are many types of witches. There are wiccans, and those who practice ceremonial magic, there are dark witches and light witches. Witches can be extremely broad and varied in terms of their perspectives, practices, and beliefs.

How to know they are around: Witches are different from the other categories in here because they are human (at least in my experience). Just like other humans, there are light witches and dark witches. This category is different because witches are human and can look just like anybody else. I have known witches that looked like fashion models and those that look like soccer moms. I have never met any with scraggly hair and a warty nose. There are witches that work a lot with plants and some that work a lot with animals and some that don't. Witches in many ways are as varied as people are as a whole. If you have a stereotype about them, it's probably wrong.

How to protect yourself: You will not need to protect yourself from a light witch, however if a witch who uses dark magic sets his or her sights on you, use shielding, protecting and clearing techniques and, by all means, ask the angels for assistance. I do not recommend counter attack as it will likely backfire on you or lead to escalation. The law of karma is very real, so anyone who sends something negative your way will suffer for it in the end. There is no need to get involved personally and then have your own nasty karma to deal with.

Where to find them: They are likely to be just about anywhere. Though there are a lot of stereotypes about witches, in my experience witches look just like other people. Sure there are some witches that might look as if they are into the occult, but in my experience that is actually the rare exception. Witches are in cities and towns, large and small, all over the country. There are witches who practice solo and there are covens. There are those who are born into families that practice witchcraft, and those who choose to practice witchcraft as an adult. Some are open about their practice while others do it privately. Since most practice witchcraft in the privacy of their own homes, you are unlikely to know if you are encountering a witch unless they are open about it. In this information age, it has never been easier to get information about practicing witchcraft and it is possible to learn a great deal on your own through books, the web, etc. which means people can be learning about and practicing witchcraft without anyone else knowing about it.

Tips: Most witches I have met look remarkably normal, so don't go looking around for a hook-nosed old woman riding a broom.

Note: Most people reading this book are more likely to have been persecuted (rightly or wrongly) as a witch in past lives. There is a great deal of fear regarding persecution from those who have had this fate in the past. The number of people killed during the witch trials is difficult to track but the estimated range is in the tens of thousands to the millions. Either way, there are a large number of people who died and were tortured after being accused of witchcraft. In many cases, there was nothing to the allegations and many healers were persecuted because of fear and misinformation that was spreading about witchcraft. If you feel this has happened to you, I recommend asking the angels to help you release any fear of persecution and heal any unhealthy patterns that led to these situations. Patterns that may need to be resolved are self-sacrificing patterns or attacking those in power in a way that is not strategic or wise. This is a complex issue and I do recommend that those who have this fear or believe they were burned or killed as witches in the past, investigate this in order to heal. This can be done through past-life regressions, readings, meditations, and psychic work to address and heal this pattern and the pain and fear it brings up in the present.

There are some dark witches who may attack you, it is more likely that witches fear other humans. In fact, many practicing witches and others who have talents in the metaphysical and natural realm like psychics and healers, have been burned as witches in the past. This has led to a lot of fear about being open with their healing and spiritual gifts and talents. I have been burned as a witch in several lifetimes and, as a result of this, I had a lot of fear to work through about being public with what I do.

While there are some real dangers that I write about in this book, some of the most dangerous creatures are humans. Sometimes the most monstrous beings don't look like monsters at all. I grew up in the gothic community and many non-goth people have expressed to me that people in the goth community frightened them because of their appearance. It's often those that look scary who are not and vice versa. Pay attention to your intuition rather than letting appearances or stereotypes be the only factor you consider in discerning whether someone or something is dangerous. Be cautious of those who wear their darkness on the inside, those are the ones you have to be really careful with. They often look just like everyone else, but pure evil lurks inside. Serial killers often look very normal.

I also feel guided to caution against sex magick or magick intended to invoke sexual power or to bring the "love" of a particular person to you. I say love in quotation marks because creating an emotional response from someone against their will is not light. It is quite easy for this type of magick to backfire. The same is true of casting curses. A curse or a hex will cause problems for both the one creating the magic and those on the receiving end. I caution against practicing either kind of magick, or asking someone else to do it on your behalf.

Most of what concerns me about witches is not witches who do dark things to humans but rather humans who do dark things to witches, or those they think are witches. It is important to discern what is safe, but too often there is an assumption of darkness or evil intent when actually there is none. A demon can make themselves look like an angel but will always feel like a demon. Pay attention, not just external indicators, but what is inside. Above all, follow your intuition.

TEN
Devil(s)

Other names: Diablo, Satan, Shaitan

What are they? Devils are incarnated dark beings described in Judaism, Christianity and Islam. They are very much master-minds of the dark. They have a more human-like quality than demons typically and are less likely to simply spontaneously attack than to make long, well-thought out plans to ensnare individuals in darkness. They command and work together with demons. They detest anything light or good simply on principle alone. They may carry out their plans over multiple lifetimes. They have long memories and may carry out personal vendettas against specific souls who have blocked or thwarted their attempts to reign and they create dark actions in humans and other incarnated beings. While some of the other beings I describe in this book (like vampires, werewolves and faeries) are incarnated, devils are in their pure form and that form is pure dark. While incarnated beings may do things that are dark, when their body dies and they go into the light, they shed the darkness and become a being of light again. Devils on the other hand, do not have light but rather are beings of darkness. For this reason, there are no benefits to communicating with them. This is true for demons also and, in many cases, demons and devils are thought to be the same thing. However, devils have a distinctly more human look and approach than many demons, in my experience. That said, much of what I said for demons also applies to devils. I do not recommend ever making a deal with either as they never make a deal that is not in their favor and when a deal is made, it rarely turns out the way the human hoped. It should be noted that there is a great deal of crossover in beliefs between devils, demons, and djinn (genies, in Western terminology). Djinn are beings made of fire that predate humans. You can read the chapter on djinn to get more details on them specifically.

How to know they are around: When devils are around or attacking, you will likely feel very psychically triggered and things will just not seem to go your way. They are masters of manipulation, so unlike lower level demons who might just physically attack or cause chaos and problems in your life, a devil will work on you psychologically to influence you to make choices that make them rejoice. The idea of an angel on one shoulder and the devil on another is recorded as far back as the 2nd century A.D. and, in my experience, this is very much how angels and devils operate. Both sides will try to encourage you to see their side and choose either the light or the darkness. Keep in mind that in the spiritual world, you are not likely to actually hear these voices unless you are very clairaudient (psychic hearing). You are more likely to hear what they say as your own thought, impression, or impulse. I have said it before but will say it again, our thoughts are almost never just our thoughts. One great way to get clarity on what is your thought and what is not, is to meditate to clear your mind and ask the angels to protect your thoughts and feelings on a regular basis. Devils thrive on getting us to choose a destructive path.

How to protect yourself: Devils are very powerful and full of trickery. Watch for alluring offers from the dark. Devils will tempt you with whatever they know will have a particular appeal for you. Ask Archangel Michael for help, clearing, and protection as well as help clearing and releasing any openings or vulnerabilities to the dark. Devils are very clever and will try to turn you against the light using logic and temptations in the physical world. Ask yourself if what you are thinking or feeling an impulse to do is loving to you and others. If it is not loving to both sides, the influence is likely coming from a devil or other dark being.

Where to find them: Devils have their own plane where they reside, but like many of the beings described in this book, they can cross into our plane and influence us. They tend to be energetic versus physical, but I believe they can manifest in the physical if they so desire, much like an angel or fallen angel. Some believe that demons and fallen angels are the same but based on my experience, they have different patterns and energy signatures so I do not feel that this is the case.

Tips: Inviting demons or devils into your life will only lead to trouble in the end. Demons and devils never make a deal that is not in their favor. Choosing light principles (love, faith, hope, peace, etc.) will help. Also, actively work to release any unhealthy patterns or behaviors that draw them in. Addiction, in particular, is a huge draw for devils. There are many forms of addiction and not just the kind that people typically think of. A person can be addicted to various substances, including the obvious, such as alcohol, and legal or illegal drugs. They can also be addicted to sugar or sugary substances, acidic food and drink, caffeine or other stimulants. A person can also be addicted to patterns and behaviors such as helping people, certain activities, pornography, sex, and even work (workaholics are so common in the United States). Any time we let addiction rule our behavior, it creates an opening for the dark and makes us easier to manipulate. If you struggle with addiction, know that it is a coping mechanism. It is important to look at what it is that we need to release, in order to be happy and fulfilled, so we don't need to cope. This is, of course, harder work in the short term but much better in the long term. Devils will often try to get us to get a "quick fix" that ultimately leads us down a long term road to destruction.

ELEVEN
Fallen Angels

Other names: The Grigori, the Watchers

What are they? Fallen angels unfortunately do exist. This is too bad since they are very powerful and all that energy used in a negative way can do major damage. In the movie *The Seventh Son*, Jeff Bridges' character says, "When you deal with the dark, the dark gets in you." And while I do not agree with the statement completely, some angels, when dealing with the darkest of the dark, sometimes get poisoned and become dark themselves. Thankfully, they are very rare and it is unlikely that anyone reading this will come into contact with one. Just like angels, they can manifest matter, and change circumstances, though in this case, those impacted by fallen angels will have bad luck rather than good. Fallen angels are in anger, pain, frustration, sadness, etc. so that is the energy that they spread to others.

How to know they are around: When fallen angels are around, they create a very specific set of symptoms including:

- Aching bones
- Strong emotional triggers
- Strange patchy goosebumps especially on the arms
- Tingling or cold sensations
- Technical problems
- Mechanical problems
- Receiving unhelpful messages through music and media
- Sad, angry, or destructive thoughts about yourself or others
- Watery eyes
- Finding hairs (especially dark hairs) even in places/ways that seem unlikely or unexplainable
- Receiving mixed messages in terms of guidance

How to protect yourself: You can ask Archangel Michael and the angels to watch over and protect you. Ask the angels to escort the fallen angel into the light for healing. Ask the angels to heal any damage done to you or loved ones and to clear away any negative energy residue left by the fallen angel.

Fallen angels are highly toxic so if you are struggling with fallen angels, you might also check in to what other areas of life you are allowing toxicity. Like attracts like, so if a fallen angel is attacking, there is something that is attracting them. It could be toxic beliefs, toxic people in your life, or toxins you are allowing in your energy field. Releasing unhealthy patterns, beliefs, relationships, food, drink, substances and environments will help you be more protected against fallen angel attacks.

With fallen angel attacks, it is also highly likely there is some kind of karma with the attacking angels. In some cases, those being attacked are incarnated angels or very high level souls with big soul missions. The stakes for the light (and the dark) are very high so they may be disproportionally targeted by fallen angels and other high level dark beings. If this is the case, looking at karma and unhealthy patterns is really important to help clear and eliminate any openings the dark has for the targeted individual.

Where to find them: Fallen angels can shift from their dimension to the human dimension so they can, in essence, be anywhere. Just like angels in the light, they can create human-looking bodies to be in or manifest physical objects, etc. in the human plane.

Tips: There is some confusion regarding the difference between a fallen angel and a demon. An angel was light in its purest form and then became dark whereas a demon was dark to begin with. However, in many ways they are handled the same. In my experience, fallen angels are more powerful and more intelligent, so if you have to deal with them, they are a force to be reckoned with.

One of the Most Serious Types of Attack

I have been told by my spirit guides that fallen angels magnify dark emotions and psychological triggers like fear, anxiety, stress, anger, etc. times 1,000 just in the same way that light angels magnify positive emotions like love, hope, faith, gratitude, etc. times 1,000. For this reason, when a fallen angel attacks, you can go from happy to hopeless and crying in a matter of moments. Any potential for stress, fear, etc. is magnified to the extreme through their manipulation.

Finding dark hairs is similar to finding feathers in unexpected places from angels of the light. As lovely as it is to find a feather in this way, it is gross or disturbing to find a hair from an unknown source. This particular phenomenon puzzled me for a while as I was finding hairs that I could not explain. I have long, blonde hair and I was regularly finding long, dark hairs in inexplicable places. For example, I might pull one out of my handbag or, stranger still, get into the bath and find several long, dark hairs in there when no one aside from me had used the bathtub or even the shower. I started to notice a pattern with other types of attacks and the hairs and made the association with fallen angels.

      Burning and watery eyes is another common indicator that you are getting attacked or targeted. I was shown that this happens because their energy is so toxic. Imagine if there was a physical toxin around you, your eyes would likely physically burn and water to clear the toxin. The same can happen with energetic toxins and fallen angels are very toxic. When your eyes are burning and watery, particularly when there is no physical source, it is very likely that a fallen angel is to blame. When this sign or other signs of fallen angels appear, ask Archangel Michael and the angels to escort these beings away from you and then try to determine how and why they attacked you. If you are very psychic, you may be able to meditate on this information to get an answer or you might hire me or another psychic who specializes in clearing fallen angels. Do inquire with the psychic as this is not a very common specialty. A psychic who is not prepared to deal with fallen angels may not help and may actually unknowingly provide misinformation.

      If you are being targeted by one or more fallen angels, your emotions will likely be very turbulent. It is highly likely that you will feel like you are on an emotional rollercoaster. Do not let this dissuade you from your path. This happens because they are trying to stop us from doing well and from making progress on our life-missions. If they can get us to voluntarily choose to stop making progress, it is much easier for them than continually trying to block us. They will attack and then let up on the attack until we start to feel hopeful again and then another round of assault will come.

Getting mixed messages, in terms of guidance and information, is another common fallen angel attack. This might happen through your own internal guidance system or through signs you receive from the world. For example, you might ask a question of your spirit guides or angels and get a mixed yes or no response. You might try to use your intuition or empathic sense to receive guidance about two different options and receive muddied or unclear feelings. When asking for signs, you might get directly opposing messages from the universe. For example, you might hear one song that says to go to a place and another that say to stay. These messages may be incredibly detailed.

Recently, I was trying to determine where to travel next and what played out next was quite comical. I was listening to the radio and I flipped the channel right when a deejay said "fly from Chicago to Las Vegas," which was exactly what I was thinking about doing. Then the radio station switched channels by itself (physically anyway) and the person talking on that radio station said, "You can't believe everything you hear." The energy of the first message resonated to me and the second one about not believing felt very dark energetically. The reason fallen angels can communicate with us like this is that the communication channels with humans are still open to them, even when they are dark. This particular sign is a big red flag that you are being targeted by fallen angels. Demons or dark entities or other dark beings are not likely to be able to reach out and communicate with you as effectively through messages like fallen angels can.

I have been told by my spirit guides that less than a thousandth of a percent of angels fall, so don't think that this is a common problem with angels. Almost all of them are amazing beings with pure lights spirits who love and support us unconditionally. Unfortunately, when they do fall, the results can be quite extreme. If you are being targeted by fallen angels, it is highly likely that you have a life-purpose that involves creating positive shifts through the world or humanity. You are also more likely to be targeted if you are an incarnated angel.

As challenging as it can be to be here, there are a lot of things that can only be experienced on the physical plane. For some angels, these temptations proved too much. They either caused them to fall and mate with human women (against their orders) or simply psychically attack those who are here. If you want to learn more about humans and angels and their offspring, you can read about the Nephilim. The Nephilim were the children of Nephilim and humans.

There are different kinds of souls on the planet. There are human souls, animal souls, faerie souls, and angel souls, just to name a few. While animal souls are more likely to incarnate as animals and humans are more likely to incarnate as humans, there is intermingling that happens for various reasons including soul lessons and experience. In terms of my understanding, an angel is not an incarnated form, however they can incarnate in other forms. I have been shown that angels have incarnated as humans and other life forms to increase the understanding between incarnated forms and angels as well as to accomplish certain missions that can be more easily done through incarnation. If you are an incarnated angel, you are more likely to be targeted by fallen angels who are jealous that you are here having a human experience because that was one of the main issues that caused many of the angels to fall to begin with. If you want to learn more about incarnated angels, you can read Doreen Virtue's book *Earth Angels*.

In addition to clearing the fallen angels who are attacking us, we must inquire as to what it is in us that is making us vulnerable to attack. When we are psychically attacked, there is always some kind of belief system or pattern which is allowing the attack. For example, we might feel sorry for those who are attacking. This is actually a dark pattern or belief because it does not honor the other individual's power or freewill choice. Feeling sorry for them disempowers the other person and is not an accurate way to view the world. Each of us is empowered to create the existence we desire through our experience and if we buy into their victim status or blame, we are affirming their lack of power, which is not correct. Another potential psychological opening is feeling that we are not worthy. We are beings of light and love with infinite potential and if we have been chosen for a particular soul mission then it is for a reason. To question this is quite dark and so even the smallest doubt about our ability to make a difference or our worthiness for the task, is a dark thought that may allow the dark to come swooping in. Once we can identify our pattern of belief which is making us vulnerable to attack, we can work with the angels to help shift and clear it so that we are no longer susceptible to that particular trigger.

This type of clearing and shifting is multi-layered so you may work on a particular subject and release one aspect of the trigger only to find another related issue rising up to be dealt with. For example, you might be working on issues of self-sacrifice. In order to heal this pattern, you have to stop giving in ways that lead to problems for you. You may also need to heal beliefs that you can't help and feel good while doing so. You will then have to shift any beliefs that you cannot feel good while helping. This is a particular challenge for light workers and incarnated angels especially as we are so focused on helping that we forget ourselves in the process. Healing and releasing these patterns is often a multi-faceted process and happens over a period of time. That said, it is possible to remove the fallen angel at the time of attack and work on the triggers they have identified. If another attack happens, it is in indicator that there is more work to be done.

TWELVE
Djinn

Other names: Jinn, genies, the hidden ones

What are they? Djinn are a type of shapeshifter and probably the most common form of shapeshifters to interact with the human realm. They are a type of being described in the Quran and widely regarded as real in the Middle East and Middle- Eastern countries, though beings with similar properties are described in cultures all over the world. In some Native American cultures, these beings are called tricksters. As with humans, the djinn has free will and can be light, dark, or grey. As with vampires, we often have dark or negative impressions, and there are plenty who warrant that reputation, but there are others who are light and kind. It is important to use your intuition when deciding whether a being has light or dark tendencies. I share information here about some of the more negative or intense aspects of human/djinn interaction because the purpose of this book is to educate, inform, and allow people to protect themselves against supernatural beings with malicious tendencies.

How to know they are around:

- Insects or animals acting strangely around you such as skunks, flies, spiders, centipedes, moths, and earwigs
- Strange dreams or trouble sleeping
- Seeing strange, shadowy visitors
- Night visitations in which the being is mating or attempting to mate with you
- Malfunctioning electronics
- Fire or electrical occurrences including fire, lightning strikes, electrical sparks, etc.
- Feeling watched and unwelcome
- Seeing strange creatures in the physical world that do not look of this world
- Feeling psychologically triggered
- Problems with romantic relationships (if a djinn gets triggered with jealousy)
- Strange weather occurrences
- Possession or attempted possession

How to protect yourself: To protect yourself from djinn, you must understand how they operate. It is important to have strong energetic and psychic boundaries. While it is possible to make a deal with a djinn in a similar as you would with a demon or devil, I really do not recommend doing so. Any short term rewards you might get would likely not be worth the price you later be asked to pay. Similarly, while it is possible to trap a djinn and force it to do your will, this approach is likely to backfire. This concept of having a genie in a bottle comes from this practice of trapping and enslaving them. I believe that the practice of enslaving something is going to cause problems for you, in this life or another, so while it may be tempting to tap into the power they possess, it rarely ends well for the person trying to do this. Not voluntarily messing with djinn is a good first step. If you find that djinn is coming to you and attempting to get involved or interfering with you, there are several things you can do to exert your authority over yourself and your domain. You must feel 'in your power' and invoke protection. Looking at past-life karma or patterns that are influencing the situation can also be helpful to understand why they are attacking and influencing you.

Since the djinn are masters of illusion, if you are attracting them into your life, you might also consider in what other areas of your life you are being fooled by illusion. In my experience, it is unlikely that you are being impacted by a djinn if there is no other illusion in your life. Ask yourself what else in your life you are not seeing. Clearing blockages in one life area will help in another. If you are not seeing things as they are with humans, you will struggle to see the truth with djinn and other supernatural creatures as well.

Tips: Since the djinn are shapeshifters, they can make us see whatever they want us to. Do not be tricked into believing that whatever they present to us is real. Follow what feels right. Also, they are not of this domain and though they often try to occupy our plane, it is not their rightful home. We have the right to say that we don't want them in our space just as you would with another human being.

Where to find them: Their dimension is on a different plane from ours but it is adjacent to ours. They have the ability to cross over ours at will. Like faeries, and angels, they are extra dimensional beings. In my experience, there are certain places that they prefer to hang out. Wilderness and deserts are the stereotype. I have noticed them in a lot of mountainous, desert-like environments like those found in the foothills of Colorado, Utah and Nevada.

History of the Djinn

It should be noted that the djinn make several appearances in the Quran and while many Middle-Easterners believe in djinn, the idea is more foreign to Westerners. Our idea of djinn is probably most influenced by the television show "I dream of Genie" than reality. While there are some nice djinn, in my experience, those that interact with humans are often not the nice variety. The story of djinn in the Quran shares that djinn were made of smokeless fire, angels made of light, and humans and other earth beings like animals are made of clay (earth). Djinn predated humans but God cast them out because they were not listening to God's will and felt themselves superior to humans. Since then, many djinn have been bent on the destruction and ruin of humanity. For those unfamiliar with the Quran, Muslims believe that the text was given to the prophet Muhammed by the Angel Gabriel (Jibril). There is some debate whether the being that communicated with Mohammed was actually an angel or a djinn masquerading as an angel. Some do not find that the behavior described (which included strangling Mohammed when he would not listen) as angelic behavior and came to the conclusion that this was not actually Gabriel. The djinn are specifically mentioned in the Quran more than 30 times.

Djinn Stories and Strange Problems

Since the djinn are beings of smokeless fire, they can easily create fires and wreak havoc with electronics and electrical devices. This could involve causing problems with cell phones, computers, lights, or just about anything that runs on power or batteries. After I had pretty well learned how to protect myself from dark entities and demons, I started to have problems with electronics etc. that were not as easy to clear. Djinn showed up for me as something to clear at a time when I was learning how to clear fallen angels. I now believe that dark djinn and fallen angels will often work together and make agreements with each other.

Since djinn are made of smokeless fire, there are many who believe them to be plasma-based beings. From this plasma state, they can easily impact electrical devices and influence weather. Recently, I was staying with a friend in Golden, Colorado. In one weekend, I had a series of incidents happen that puzzled me at first. Later I understood how they were connected, through the djinn. There was a wildfire at North Table Mountain in Golden which was only about a mile from where I was staying. That same day, two smoke alarms started beeping as if their batteries were low, but they were doing so irregularly. When the battery goes out, the beeping usually starts and then keeps going, but this was not the case. The smoke detectors would beep 15, 30 minutes or sometimes hours apart but always when I was in a different part of the house so I could not identify which smoke detector was the culprit. The beeping completely stopped around the time the fire was contained and did not start again. I felt this was them playing with me a little, starting a fire and then messing with the devices that would notify me of a fire in the building.

While staying with the same friend, I had a series of problems with the garage door openers and the garage door. In several cases, I could not get the garage door to open upon returning home. One evening, I nearly spent the night in the car when the garage door opener in one car would not work. I was stuck outside with the garage door closed. I tried it about 50 times and then decided to try one more time before sleeping in the car. I figured I would have to get a new battery for the opener because I thought that was the problem. Interestingly, I also had my phone break a few days before. The code to the garage door that you could type in to manually open the door was in my broken phone but not in the new one. I asked the angels to help me and miraculously, the garage door opener worked on my last attempt. I thanked the angels and went inside with relief. When my friend returned from out of town, I told him what had happened and he went and replaced the battery. A different day, I was driving a different car with a different garage door opener and the same thing happened. I now believe the battery had nothing to do with anything and it was the djinn messing with the devices, trying to keep me from getting inside.

In a separate incident at a different residence, the smoke detector also went off in the middle of the night. I took the battery out, unattached it from the house power supply and still had to put the smoke detector in the garage in order to be able to sleep. There is no physical way that it should have continued to beep and yet it did.

I had a client who had something similar happen with a malfunctioning garage door opener and garage door. She had problems with the garage door not closing when she was trying to leave the house. After months of it working intermittently, she purchased a new one for a few hundred dollars and had it reinstalled. It worked well for a couple of months and then the same thing started to happen. When you have recurring problems, even after you have replaced the "broken" item, it is likely not a physical problem but rather something interfering. Djinn, dark entities, demons and fallen angels will cause problems like this. It should be noted that sometimes, if they have messed with a device enough, it may need to be replaced as it may not function properly any longer. That said, replacing the item without removing whatever is causing the malfunction can get to be a very expensive and frustrating process that allows the problem to continue.

While at a client's home that had a lot of djinn activity, I was amazed that several times I plugged my phone in to charge only to wake up or return and find it unplugged. I rely on my phone a lot for business as well as for personal matters and so this was annoying, but I persisted and asked the angels to protect the phone and the charger and after that, it remained plugged in after I connected the phone to the charger. As with entities, if there are djinn that are not happy with your presence, they will do whatever they can to get a rise out of you. If you stay calm and don't get frustrated, they will likely stop doing that particular activity as often, their goal is to frustrate or get a reaction from you.

As I have learned about different supernatural creatures and how to manage them, I have also learned how to protect myself from each one. I think of it like levels of initiation or leveling up. When you play a video game and you level up, not only do the rewards get bigger but the bad guys do too and it's similar with life. Though I have historically had phone problems due to entity attacks, once I learned how to clear them, I had a period of time where my phone and computer (which had also been targeted) were less problematic. Then suddenly I had a series of problems with phones leading to the need to purchase 3 new phones within a period of 3 months because of strange malfunctions, not caused by physical damage. I believe this was due to djinn attacks as I was not protected from dark entities and demons. By learning how djinn attack and determining what was attacking, I was able to clear and ask for protection for my devices, etc. This same pattern happened with my electronics when I was learning how to deal with dark entities and demons.

Another sign that you may have djinn nearby is finding or seeing lots of dead animals around. This may be on the road or around your house. At one client's home that had a large djinn presence, they were finding dead animals in the area on an almost daily basis.

Similarly, finding skunks and smelling particularly bad smells can also be an indicator of djinn. In one instance, at a client's home with djinn activity, there were skunks regularly present and sometimes spraying. In one day, the client's dog was sprayed and later that evening, a skunk sprayed in the same vicinity. I believe this is because they are wanting to make it unpleasant for people and are trying to get them to leave. Certain demons and dark entities can also spray and smell very bad though, in my experience, there is usually a different quality to the smell. Demons and dark entities usually smell like decay, rotting, or putrefaction whereas djinn will create smells that are acrid or sour but also intense. It is also possible that both are in the same area. There is definitely cross-over with attributes to djinn and some demons or dark entities, but I do feel they are different energy signatures. After dark entities and demons no longer seemed to be able to impact me, the djinn were able to do so until I learned how to protect myself from them, leading me to believe they are, in fact, a different type of being.

Types of Djinn

A marid is thought to be one of the more powerful types of djinn. They are very smart and are most associated with granting wishes to humans.

Ifrit, also spelled afrit or efreet, is another very powerful type of djinn. In some instances, the words marid and ifrit are used seemingly interchangeably. They are depicted with enormous wings and are said to live underground and sometimes in ruins. Their depiction is often very similar to the Western idea of a traditional demon or devil. They are shown with horns, red and within fire.

Ghul are a type of ghoulish djinn who drink blood and feast on human flesh. They are said to inhabit graveyards and other quiet and creepy places. They are referenced in *1001 Arabian Nights.*

Hinn are a type of djinn that are not considered as intelligent as some other forms and often take the appearance of dogs.

Iblis, said to be the leader of the djinn, is the most powerful of them all and is often equated with the Western idea of the devil. In the Quran, Iblis is described as stating his superiority over Adam, who was made from clay, and Iblis and other djinn, from fire. God then cursed Iblis to Hell but granted him purgatory until judgement day. Since that day, Iblis has made it his mission to destroy humanity.

Jann are shapeshifting djinn who are intelligent and associated with the desert. They are associated with whirlwinds and white camels. The ghul and the jann do not get along.

Qarins are a type of djinn that is believed to be accompanying each person. The plural form is qareen. The direct translation means constant companion. There seem to be two ideas about the qarin, one is that they can be equated to the Western idea of a devil on your shoulder, encouraging you to do bad things. The other is that they can be more light, but if their human goes dark, they do too. A quarin can be of either gender, but if they are the opposite gender to their human, they can fall in love with their human companion and try to destroy any relationships their human tries to have.

Palis is a type of djinn who are called foot lickers as they are known to drain people of blood by licking their feet.

Shaitan or Shaytan is a very dark, evil djinn who is associated with malevolent forces. In some cases, they are listed as synonymous with Iblis. This is the source for the English word for Satan. Shaitan is described as the whisperer who can whisper urges to sin to both humans and djinn.

Deals with Humans

Similar to demons or devils, one of the interactive patterns with humans is that humans can make deals with them. Just as with demons and devils, the deal rarely turns out as the human expects and there are often severe and negative consequences that result from the deal. Djinn can also be enslaved, bound to objects and used by humans for their purposes but again, this usually backfires (that is karma in my opinion). The most famous example of this is King Solomon.

King Solomon was the King of Israel approximately 970-931 BC and he is credited with building the first Temple of Jerusalem. Legend says that he imprisoned djinn to help build the temple using a magic ring that gave him power over them. Eventually, one of the djinn was able to get the ring and cast out Solomon, leaving him destitute. Eventually, Solomon was able to get the ring back and he imprisoned the djinn in a bottle. He is also rumored to have had a love affair with the Queen of Sheba who was reported to be half djinn.

Jealousy

Djinn will often fall in love with and desire humans and can become obsessive. If the human they are interested in starts to have a relationship with someone, they will get jealous and do everything in their power to destroy the relationship.
Since they are shapeshifters, they can make themselves appear as they wish. I once had a friend email me and describe a visitation in which I was there but not there and he felt that he was having sex with me. After doing research and learning about the djinn, I now believe it was a djinn that was masquerading as me. They will take whatever form they believe will arouse us. Note that no matter how enticing and beautiful they appear to be, they are not that way in their true form and their true form would more likely horrify you than turn you on.

    I was visiting with a friend recently and we were watching a movie. Half-way through the movie, my friend called out for me and asked what was going on. When I looked psychically, I was shocked to see a large moth-like humanoid creature on her in a mating position. She had felt something odd and a vibration which I assume was from the creature's wings which were moving at a very fast pace. There are certain dimensions or beings which I will not immediately see unless I am focusing clairvoyantly and since I was focused on the movie, I hadn't been paying attention. But as soon as I saw the creature, I asked the angels for clearing and protection. It was clear this creature was displaying aggression and claiming territory over my friend. I had learned that my friend had just started seeing someone new and there had been clear sabotage attempts made on the relationship. Moths and moth-like creatures are often associated with djinn and some believe that the moth man who appeared in Point Pleasant, North Virginia in 1966 and 1967 was a djinn. The moth man was described as a man with ten-foot wings seen flying around in the vicinity. Many later associated a local bridge collapse with the Moth Man. After the collapse, there were no more sightings.

Insects and The Djinn

Generally, I am a fan of animals large and small and am friendly to most insects, but right around the time I started noticing some other djinn signs, I started to be plagued by insects that were not acting normally and that felt dark and creepy. Often times, I find insects to be wonderful animal messengers and welcome their presence, but in these cases, their presence felt dark and manipulative somehow. Spiders that normally feel like reminders to write and manifest felt like they were spying on me. They started to show up consistently in my room and in the house where I was staying. While I would normally catch a spider and put it outside, I distinctly got the message to kill these spiders. I am unclear whether these spiders and other insects were being possessed and used by the djinn or whether they were actually physically manifested by the djinn for their purposes.

I have had several other strange experiences with earwigs that did not feel right. In one case, I had just returned from a trip to New Orleans and was unpacking my suitcase. I pulled out a sequined dress and there was an earwig on it. It was a very strange place for an earwig and once again it did not feel natural. On another trip in Park City, Utah, I found 3 earwigs in the period of 3 minutes. In the first instance, the earwig was on the bathroom counter and was facing me with his back end pointed at me in an aggressive fashion. I killed him and then promptly there was another one in my toiletry bag. A few minutes later when I walked into my bedroom, a third earwig was next to my suitcase. A few minutes later, I saw a very strange looking spider in the bathroom. In each case, they felt like they were watching me and were not friendly and seemed somewhat ominous in energy. Later that evening, there was an incredible lightning storm outside. This client's home had also been struck by lightning when she had first moved in.

When I was first learning about djinn, a friend of mine told me she was struggling with djinn and with strange insect behavior. In particular, she described a centipede that was in her house on her wall. It was not a house centipede but one that you typically find outside. This is odd behavior for a centipede. So if you are noticing insects in large numbers or that are acting strangely around you, you may have a djinn problem. Again, insects that are associated with djinn are spiders, flies, earwigs, centipedes or millipedes, and moths.

How to Clear Djinn

Here are some tips I have been given to clear the djinn:

- Ask the angels to clear any djinn and protect you. Do this in general and if you are experiencing any potential djinn at the moment of encounter.

- Ask the angels to clear their energy or spies (they often will use insects to gain information on us).
- Break any agreements or deals you may have made with a djinn in all direction of time. Deals from other lifetimes can carry over into this one until they are cleared.
- Tell the djinn (out loud or in your head) that you do not want the djinn around or influencing you and ask the angels for help enforcing boundaries.
- Practice strong personal boundaries. Our actions show what really want so if we say one thing but do another, the action will always override the thought. If you say you do not want djinn in your life, but you let people walk all over you, the message to the universe is that you want people to take advantage of you and the djinn are more than happy to follow suit.
- Ask to see things clearly as they are in all areas of your life. Falling for illusion with humans will likely mean that you will get caught up in illusion with djinn as well.

As with any type of attack, I recommend clearing any psychological and energetic openings and then determining if you are in a place that has a lot of activity. If so, it may be advisable to leave the location to protect yourself. This is something you will have to decide on a case by case basis. If you have very strong boundaries, you may be able to clear or protect yourself from certain beings while others may overwhelm you in which case leaving the area is advised. Of course, there is always the possibility that certain beings will follow you if you go. If this happens, getting professional help from a shaman, psychic medium, or another expert is recommended.

THIRTEEN
Zombies

Other names: Zombi, zonbi, the undead, the living dead, the walking dead

What are they? Zombies are actually the one creature here that may strike the most terror but are not currently real in the supernatural sense as far as I am aware. Yes, it is possible through certain herbs and plants to create a zombie (as some voodoo queens have been known to do). This is not a supernatural effect but rather a side effect of certain substances. That said, this is the type of creature that I have the least amount of personal experience with. In the Haitian culture, a zombie is a reanimated corpse brought to life with magic. In modern pop culture, such as movies and television, zombies are often created through some kind of medical epidemic. Characteristics of zombies include:

- Mindless and feral behavior
- Insatiable hunger for human flesh and brains specifically
- Inability to feel pain or emotions
- Lack of ability to think critically
- Focus purely on satiating hunger and destroying anything that gets in the way of this

How to know they are around: You will know if they are around when there is a total societal breakdown and you are being chased by zombies! But in truth, there are biological agents or diseases such as neurotropic viruses or prions that could target the brain and create zombie-like creatures, but to date, nothing widespread has been discovered that would create a pandemic as is often portrayed in film and television. Prions are infectious protein particles which were responsible for Mad Cow Disease in the 1990s. Rabies is a more known virus that causes those infected to go crazy and bite others, passing on the infection. Fifty-five thousand people a year still die from rabies which is pretty mind-boggling (1 person every 10 seconds).

Where to find them: In the event of a zombie apocalypse, zombies can be anywhere humans are. That said, if zombies are created through disease or some kind of pathogen, then they will likely be in high concentrations in cities and the chance of survival would likely be higher in rural or less populated regions. During the bubonic plague, people fled the cities in an attempt to escape the pandemic. The plague killed 50 million people and it is estimated that as much as 60% of the population of Europe died in the 14th century alone, and that was just one of several outbreaks.

How to protect yourself: In the event of an actual zombie apocalypse, get to a safe space, away from others and ensure you have weapons and access to safe food and water. And of course, always ask the angels for protection and run as fast as you can away from them. If zombies are being created through some kind of contagion, then I recommend calling on Archangel Raphael for healing. Archangel Michael is a badass and always good to call on for any kind of danger and protection.

Tips: In the event of a zombie apocalypse, it seems to me that the soul is either not in charge or is completely absent. Be wary of anything without an empathy response. It is unclear what happens to the soul if someone becomes a zombie. It feels to as if it's highly likely the soul wanders, similar to a ghost but with a body that is technically alive but not an appropriate vehicle for a soul any longer.

Haitian Zombies

When we look at zombies historically, we often first look to those created by shamans. They are very different than pop culture zombies that were typically created for the purposes of manual labor. The process involved a Boker (a voodoo priest or shaman) who cursed the individual and then it is believed that they captured the soul and thereby entrapped the person in their control. In the Haitian culture, zombis of zonbis (traditional Haitian spelling) are usually sympathized with rather than feared because they are victims. This is quite a difference from what mainstream Americans think of when they think of zombies. A zombi likely moves slowly, has a gray pallor, and can only say very rudimentary things. So while the term zombi comes from Haiti and is connected with voodoo, similarities to a more current idea of a zombie are actually pretty minimal aside from the fact that they are not in charge of their full mental capacities.

Zombie Depictions in Pop Culture, Movies and Television

Classic horror stories that include zombie-like creatures include *Frankenstein* by Mary Shelley and later *I Am Legend,* a novel written by Richard Matheson in 1954 and adapted into a movie four different times. *White Zombie,* a movie featuring famed horror actor Bela Lugosi, was released in 1932, but the big zombie revolution and renaissance was sparked by the 1968 movie *Night of the Living Dead*. Then came *Dawn of the Dead*, *Day of the Dead*, and *Return of the Living Dead*. Later, the pop culture zombie contagion spread to television shows like *World War Z, The Walking Dead,* and *Z Nation*. Another wave of movies about zombies came with *World War Z* and *Shaun of the Dead*. I find it fascinating to note just how interested people are with zombies. In addition to a resurgence in movies and television about zombies, there are now zombie crawls or walks all over the country in which thousands of people get dressed up as zombies.

Zombie-like Creatures in Mythology and World Cultures

Though the term zombie has only come to be used within the last two hundred years or so, there are zombie like creatures that have been described in various world cultures and mythologies. There are many that are undead and are described as zombie-like and potentially vampiric. These include the Romanian legend of the Strigoi, a troubled, undead spirit that rises from the dead. The Albanian term Shtriga is for a vampiric and witch-like creature that also drinks blood. Jiangshi are Chinese zombie creatures are described in their mythology. Wights are another type of animated corpse -the name comes from Middle English which means thing. Another similar creature is a Lich or Leiche in German. This creature, however, is thought to be more intelligent than a zombie.

Real Zombies

In many ways, I do think that zombies are real, but not in the way that you might think. I believe we are living in a sort of zombified culture in which many people are acting like zombies. Something I have witnessed is that a good part of our society is living their life in a zombified way. Here are some of the traits of zombies that I feel are very prevalent in society right now:

- Focused only on physical needs
- Emotionless
- Not working cooperatively
- Short term thinking
- Lacking goals, dreams, or plans
- Using force, instead of critical thinking to get what they want
- Focusing purely on meeting base physical needs

I feel that many people are shoving down their emotions and coping through substances like food or drugs that they feel they need. As a people, we are not as cooperative as we used to be. In many cases, people are isolated and do not have community. I also see patterns in terms of many people orienting themselves to short term gratification and not planning for long term. People often make choices that are about convenience and pain avoidance rather than using critical thinking skills to make good long term decisions. We have also gotten into an age of might versus right meaning whoever is the strongest or has the largest army is the right party. These are exaggerations but I sometimes wonder if our fascination as a culture with zombies is because there is something that really hits home for us about them. The idea of losing ourselves and becoming mindless monsters who focus only on flesh is terrifying but can also be looked at as an analogy for losing our souls and living from a purely physical perspective. It seems appropriate to share a quote from Guillermo Del Toro, the famed horror screenwriter and director who said, "The real monsters in our lives are in fancy tailored suits." Something to remember is that often times the real monsters don't look like monsters at all.

Afterword

My intention for this book was to shed some light on a world that many humans are not aware of or think of only in a fictional context. I believe that we are entering into a time when many illusions are going to be shattered and the truth will be revealed. Though the realization that many of these beings are real may frighten many people, remember their real-ness is not new, just the perception of them is new. If you get caught up in fear as your sense of reality shifts, ask the angels to help you release any fear and protect you. Only when we know what is real and what is illusion can we truly protect ourselves and navigate effectively. One benefit to understanding that the world is filled with the paranormal is that it also means magic is real. It means you are more powerful than you ever imagined and while that too may seem scary, you are capable of so much more than you ever dreamed. Open your eyes to mystery, magic, and the real world as you've never seen it before.

Sending you love and magic,
Laura Powers

Helpful Terms/Glossary

Angel – A divine energy being. An angel is a spiritual being of light whose purpose is to guide and assist incarnated beings. The word means messenger and one of their main purposes is to take our messages to and from heaven. They are also tasked with helping us with our life and life's work.

Angel Communicator – Someone who can communicate through one or more senses (sight, hearing, feeling) with angels.

Angelic Hierarchy (also called Celestial Hierarchy) – The hierarchy classifies the angels into specific ranks and orders which relate to the duties of that particular angel type. The most commonly referred to was created by Pseudo Dionysius, the Areopagite (member of a tribunal in Athens), a philosopher and Christian mystic.

Archangels – One of the orders of angels just above the angels in the Celestial Hierarchy. They have specialty areas and work more than the higher orders.

Ascended Master – A person who lived, experienced enlightenment, and ascended so that they no longer need to incarnate for purposes of spiritual growth. Jesus and Buddha are two well-known ascended masters.

Attachments – Short for spirit or entity attachments. This is when a spiritual being energetically attaches itself to an incarnated individual (like a human or animal) and feeds on them parasitically.

Celestial Hierarchy (also called Angelic Hierarchy) – The hierarchy classifies the angels into specific ranks and orders which relate to the duties of that particular angel type. The hierarchy most commonly referred to was created by Pseudo Dionysius who was a philosopher and Christian mystic.

Cherubim – The second highest order of angels in the hierarchy is described in the Old Testament many times. They are said to have guarded the Tree of Life in Eden with a flaming sword.

Clairalience – Clear smelling or receiving information from your sense of smell, also called clairescence. This is a form of extra sensory perception or ESP.

Clairaudient – Clear hearing or hearing sounds that are not just on the physical plane. This can be hearing a sound with your ears or hearing the word or phrase in your mind like a thought which isn't yours. This is a form of extra sensory perception or ESP.

Claircognizance – Clear knowing or knowing something you have no logical way of knowing. This is a form of extra sensory perception or ESP.

Clairgustance – The ability to taste something that you have not put in your mouth. This is a form of extra sensory perception or ESP.

Clairsentience – Clear feeling or feeling something that is coming from outside of you. This can be a physical sensation or emotion. This is a form of extra sensory perception or ESP.

Clairvoyance – Clear seeing or seeing something that is not in the physical plane. Clairvoyance can be experienced with your physical eyes or with your third or internal eye. This is a form of Extra Sensory Perception or ESP.

Clearing – Releasing and clearing energy and spirit or entity attachments.

Compulsion – When a vampire uses their magical ability to magnetize a person and get them to do something against their will.

Cord – An energetic connection between people, places, and things which transmits energy and emotions.

Cryptids – An animal that cryptozoologists believe is real but is not documented or unproven.

Cryptozoology – The study of animals that are from folklore or are unknown. Some people believe it's a pseudoscience.

Demon – A supernatural energy being that feeds on and creates darkness in the world. This is a term often used within the context of religion.

Devil – A dark and malevolent leader of hell and demons. This term is usually used within a Judeo-Christian context.

Djinn – A smokeless being made of fire that is extradimensional but can shift and manifest in the human plane as well.

Dragons – A magical and mythical serpent-like creature.

Empathy – The ability to feel what others are feeling. This is a form of Extra Sensory Perception or ESP.

Energy body – The energetic part of our body; we are made of matter and energy, and both parts come together to form us.

Entity – An energetic being that does not have a physical form. Entities are non-human and are not animals or angels either but another type of being. There are many different types of entities.

EVPs (Electronic Voice Phenomenon) – Electronic recordings that are believed to have been caused by paranormal activity.

Extra dimensional – Being from a different dimension than our own. By comparison, extra-terrestrial beings are from our dimension but not from our planet.

Extra Sensory Perception (ESP) – One or more heightened senses that perceive more than the normal range of sensing.

Fallen Angels – Angels that have fallen into darkness and are no longer beings of love and light. Some people confuse them with demons.

Faeries/fairies – A type of extra-dimensional being that can come to the human plane as well. They used to share our plane but retreated to a different plane after interactions with humans led to violence and bloodshed. They are elemental beings and are associated with nature and safeguarding plants and animals.

Funhouse effect – A certain quality dreams can have when they are impacted by entities.

Ghosts – An earth bound spirit or the spirit of a person whose body had died and whose soul or spirit has not crossed into the light.

Glamouring – When a vampire uses their magical ability to magnetize a person and get them to do something against their will.

Infestation – According to the Catholic Church, infestation is the first precursor to possession in which demonic activity is occurring in the environment.

Magic/magick – The use of supernatural forces to influence outcomes.

Medium – Someone who can communicate with ghosts (earth bound spirits) and spirits (people without a body that are not earth bound).

NAET™ – Stands for Nambudripad's Allergy Elimination Technique, a method using acupuncture to eliminate allergies.

Nephilim – The children of angels and humans. They are discussed in the apocryphal Book of Enoch.

Obsession – According to the Catholic Church, obsession is the third precursor to possession in which the targeted individual is seduced or terrorized by the dark in order to allow full on possession.

Oppression – According to the Catholic Church, the second precursor to possession in which demonic activity is targeted at a specific person.

Out-of-body experience (OBE) – A phenomenon in which an individual experiences their soul separating from their body. Usually the individual will then witness their body separately from them. The soul can then travel freely without the physical limitations of the body.

Paranormal – Events that are outside the realm of normal experience and cannot be explained by current science.

Possession – According to the Catholic Church, the final level of demonic influence in which the targeted individual is fully controlled by a demon that has taken over the person's body.

Powers – An order of angels, sometimes called The Authorities. They are warrior angels and are said to act as an elite guard against dark forces.

Precognition – Knowing something is going to happen before it does with no logical way of knowing this. This is a form of Extra Sensory Perception or ESP.

Psychometry – The ability to receive information from an object through touch.

Precognition – Knowing something is going to happen before it does with no logical way of knowing this. This is a form of Extra Sensory Perception or ESP.

Principalities – (Called Archai by some) They give blessings to the material world. They inspire people in the realms of art and science and are educators.

Psychic – Someone who receives information from the non-physical world.

Psychic Medium – A psychic who communicates with spirits and other beings.

Sage – A plant that can be used to clear negative or stagnant energy.

Seraphim – The highest order of angels. The name Seraphim means the burning ones. The Ethiopian, Greek, and Hebrew words for Seraphim, translate as serpent, snake, or dragon. It is said that four Seraphim surround God and they burn from love.

Spirit – The non-physical manifestation of a person or being. The spirit never dies and is made of energy.

Supernatural – Not related to the natural or physical world.

Telepathy – The ability to communicate with others through thoughts.

Thrones – The third highest order of angels (also called The Orphanim by some). The Thrones are described as being a wheel within a wheel and covered with eyes and emanating light.

Ultra-terrestrial – Similar to the term extra-dimensional, being from a different dimension but appearing on our planet.

Vampires – Supernatural beings that feed on energy or blood. Though they look human, they are very magical and have many abilities that humans do not have such as flying, glamouring people, erasing memories, and healing.

Virtues – An order of angels who oversee the movement of the heavens.

Zombies – A reanimated human corpse created by either supernatural or medical means.

Recommended Resources/Reading List

Akashic Records: Case Studies of Past Lives by Lois Wetzel chronicles the Akashic readings of 30 clients.

Angel Numbers 101 by Doreen Virtue introduces the idea that angels communicate with us through numbers.

Angels in my Hair by Lorna Byrne shares the story of one Angel Communicator's journey coming to terms with her gift.

Animal Spirit Guides by Steven Farmer discusses animal spirit guides and related topics such as totem animals.

Ask Your Guides by Sonia Choquette gives great and practical information about how to communicate with your spirit guides.

Bringing Your Soul to Light by Dr. Linda Backman provides an exploration of the soul journey through the past and between life regressions.

Ghosts Among Us by Van Praagh is an informative book that sheds light in an informative and enlightening way on the potentially spooky subject of ghosts.

*I Had the Strangest Dream b*y Kelly Sullivan Walden is a dream analysis book that has a modern approach and word meanings that don't appear in some other dream analysis books.

Journey of Souls: Case Studies of Life Between Lives by Michael Newton takes a fascinating look at our lives between lives. Newton methodically regressed patients and noted descriptions and stories of the afterlife, revealing a surprisingly ordered system for those who are in spirit form.

Outwitting the Devil by Napolean Hill is a book written as an actual conversation with the devil about how he influences people.

Positive Energy: Ten Extraordinary Prescriptions for Transforming Fatigue, Stress, and Fear into Vibrance, Strength and Love by Dr. Judith Orloff gives practical tips for better managing your energy.

Psychic Vampire Codex: A Manual of Magick and Energy Work by Michelle A. Belanger. This book gives some great tools and tips for managing energy and energy healing work. Do not be scared by the word vampire in the title.

Sacred Signs: Hear, See and Believe Messages from the Universe by Adrian Calabrese gives simple and easy to follow guidelines on how to ask for and receive signs from your angels and spirit guides.

Second Sight by Judith Orloff, M.D. chronicles Dr. Orloff's personal journey as an intuitive and healer. She is a psychiatrist who initially turned away from her gift but gradually learned to embrace it.

The Four Agreements: A Practical Guide to Personal Freedom (A Toltec Wisdom Book) by Don Miguel Ruiz gives four suggestions for living based on Toltec Wisdom.

The World of Archangels by Sufian Chaudhary shares detailed information about the archangels and different dimensions.

A Time for Truth by Nick Bunick addresses and documents the presence of angels in the author's life but also discusses important changes within Christianity over time.

Whose Stuff is This? Finding Freedom from the Thoughts, Feelings, and Energy of Those Around You by Yvonne Perry describes one woman's journey as an empath. It is an excellent resource for those who are empathic or clairsentient.

You Are Psychic: The Art of Clairvoyant Reading and Healing by Debra Lynne Katz addresses many tools you yourself can learn to heal yourself and others.

Your Soul's Plan: A book by Robert Schwartz explores the premise that we all create a life-plan before we are born.

Recommended Movies and Television Shows

American Horror Story: A horror-based drama with each season having a different theme such as medical experimentation, witches, ghosts, and other paranormal activity.

Beautiful Creatures: A movie about a spell caster or witch who will be chosen as either dark or light on her 16th birthday. It is based on the book by the same name.

Beetlejuice: A movie about a couple who become ghosts through an accident and continue to occupy their home when a new family purchases it. The movie is named for the supernatural creature, Beetlejuice who offers to help the couple reclaim their home in his own unique way.

Blade: A movie about a vampire-human hybrid who is also a vampire slayer attempting to wipe out the vampire race.

Cinderella (2015): This live-action Disney movie tells the story of an orphaned girl who is abused by her mother and step-sisters. Her fairy godmother gives her the wonderful opportunity to have a magical night out at the Prince's ball.

City of Angels: This film tells the story of an angel who falls in love with a human he sees. He opts to forego his experience as an angel to become a mortal in order to be with her.

Constantine: A movie about a demon hunter who is dealing with demons and angels and trying to solve the mystery of the murder of a very psychic twin. This film was based on *Hellblazer* by DC Comics.

Dark Shadows: A film inspired by an earlier television show. The story centers around a witch who turns a lover who has spurned her into a vampire and then entombs him. He escaped two centuries later and comes back to his estate which has fallen into ruin and is occupied by his descendants.

Defending Your Life: A film in which the premise is that after you die you have to defend your life choices in order to ascend.

Ghost: A movie about a man who is murdered and must work through a psychic to try to warn and protect his love from his shady business partner and his associates.

Ghostbusters (1984): A movie about a group of scientists who battle evil as it is unleashed upon New York City via the paranormal.

Ghostbusters (2016): A movie about a group of paranormal investigators who get caught in an epic battle of good and evil taking place in Manhattan.

Grimm: A television drama that follows a Grimm descendent, a family line of supernatural hunters, as he deals with various mythological and storybook monsters and creatures.

High Spirits: A film about a hotel owner who creates a false rumor that his hotel is haunted to generate publicity and business. When two actual ghosts arrive, things get interesting.

Hotel Transylvania: A children's animated movie about a hotel for monsters in Transylvania. When a human unwittingly stumbles into the hotel, the monsters desperately try to hide what they are.

Hotel Transylvania 2: A sequel that tells the story of the monster hotel after it opens to humans. The storyline also followed the birth of a half-vampire, half-human child as he develops.

I am Legend: A movie that follows a scientist as he tries to create a cure for a plague that has caused people to turn into vampiric, zombie-like creatures.

It's a Wonderful Life: A movie that features the protagonist, George Bailey, after he wishes he had never been born. An angel appears and shows him how things would have been different if he had never been born.

Legend (1985): A movie about the struggle between good and evil. A demon tries to create eternal darkness through the death of the last unicorns.

Legion: A film depicting a modern day battle between angels and the forces of evil.

Let the Right One In (2008) or *Lat den ratte komma in*: A movie about the story of a boy and the new friend he develops. As the story unfolds, we learn the friend is connected to a series of grisly murders with paranormal aspects.

Maleficent: The Disney live action retelling of how Maleficent from Sleeping Beauty became who she was. She is a faerie who is peaceful until she is betrayed and the forest is destroyed.

Medium: A television show that tells the story of Allison Dubois who uses her psychic abilities to help solve crimes through her work at the District Attorney's office.

Michael: A comedic movie about a man who claims he is an angel but he does not act like a stereotypical angel.

Mortal Instruments, City of Bones: A movie about a teenage girl who learns she is a half-angel warrior. Once she learns the truth, she is immersed in a world of demons, vampires, and other supernatural creatures.

Penny Dreadful: An hour-long drama series, set in 19th century Britain, about vampires, witches, werewolves, and all manner of supernatural creatures.

Practical Magic: A movie about two sisters who have mostly avoided magic until one of them gets into a bad situation with an abusive boyfriend and they use magic to try to help.

Rosemary's Baby: A movie that takes place in New York City about a woman who gets pregnant with a child of questionable origins.

Stardust: A movie that takes place in a fairy tale world about a star (depicted as a woman) who falls from the sky and the struggle for power around her.

Supernatural: A television show that follows two brothers, Sam and Dean Winchester, as they hunt various supernatural creatures. They deal with angels and the strange happenings that unfold around them.

Teen Wolf: A television show about a teenage boy who is attacked by a werewolf and transforms himself. He tries to live a normal teenage life which is almost impossible once be becomes a part of the supernatural world.

The Conjuring: A movie inspired by paranormal investigators Ed and Lorraine Warren and a case at a farmhouse owned by the Perron family in 1970.

The Conjuring 2: A movie inspired by paranormal investigators Ed and Lorraine Warren and a possible possession case in 1977 London.

The Devil's Advocate: A movie about an attorney who accepts a job at a high level New York law firm. As he gets more involved in the firm, he begins to think there are dark, evil forces at work.

The Exorcist: A movie based loosely on actual events involving the possession of a young girl. An expert is brought in from the church to perform an exorcism.

The Gift (2000): A movie about a psychic who is asked to help find a missing woman.

The Ghost Whisperer: A television show about a woman who can see and communicate with ghosts. She does what she can to try to help them.

The Lord of the Rings Series: A movie series, based on JRR Tolkien's books, that takes place in the realm of wizards, elves, dragons, and other supernatural creatures. There is an epic battle between good and evil, centered around a group of powerful rings.

The Others: A movie about a woman who moves her family to the coast during World War II. A series of strange supernatural events plague them and it becomes clear something supernatural is happening.

The Prophecy: A movie about the battle between dark angel Gabriel and the light angel who attempts to thwart him.

The Rite: A movie about a student who attends the Vatican School of Exorcism and hears the story of a veteran exorcist which alters his belief in reality.

The Sixth Sense: A movie about a boy who sees ghosts and his relationship with the psychiatrist who helps him work through how to handle them.

The Twilight Series: A movie series centered around Bella, a teenage girl in the Pacific Northwest, and her involvement with vampires and werewolves.

True Blood: A television series that takes place in the southern United States and centers around vampires, werewolves, faeries, and other supernatural creatures. It is loosely based on the book series created by Charlaine Harris.

Underworld Series: Movies about the clash throughout history between the vampires and the lycans (werewolves).

Van Helsing: A movie about Gabriel Van Helsing, a famous hunter who is hired to kill Dracula and his associates. He combines forces with a woman named Anna to defeat the monsters.

What Dreams May Come: A movie about a man who dies and is in heaven. When his wife commits suicide, he decides to go to hell to try and rescue her soul, a task that proves more difficult than he imagined.

Jesus in India: This Paul David documentary looks at Jesus' missing years between the ages of 12 and 30 and explores the possibility that he went to the East. Historical evidence is examined and experts all over the world are interviewed.

Something Unknown is Doing We Don't Know What: A documentary that examines various phenomena such as telekinesis, precognition, and energy healing.

Thrive: A fascinating film that looks at many seemingly unrelated structures and systems such as banking, the energy industry, and health care, and strives to get us to look at our role in the system differently.

What the Bleep Do We Know?: Interviews with scientists and authors, animated bits, and a storyline involving a deaf photographer are used in this docudrama to illustrate the link between quantum mechanics, neurobiology, human consciousness, and day-to-day reality.

Sources

These are books and websites that I referenced for this book and that have informed me and my work:

20,000 Names Around the World. *Dragon Names*. 2016. http://www.20000-names.com/dragon_names.htm

360 Cities. Nine Dragon Bridge Yan an Elevated Road. 2016. http://www.360cities.net/image/nine-dragon-bridge-pillar-yan-an-elevated-road-shanghai-china

9 News. Wildfire Burning on North Table Mountain. 2016. http://www.9news.com/news/local/wildfires/wildfire-burning-on-north-table-mountain/279994556

About.com. *All About EVP*. 2014. http://paranormal.about.com/od/ghostaudiovideo/a/All-About-EVP.htm

Allen, Sue. *Spirit Release*. John Hunt Publishing. 2010.

Ancient Symbols. Dragon Symbolism. 2016. http://www.ancient-symbols.com/dragon-symbolism.html

Baring-Gould, Baring. *The Book of Werewolves*. Forgotten Books 2008.

Belanger, Jeff. *Encyclopedia of Haunted Places*. Castle Books. 2009.

Belanger, Michelle. *Dictionary of Demons: Names of the Damned.* Llewellyn Publications, 2010.

Belanger, Michelle. *Haunting Experiences: Encounters with the Otherworldly.* Llewellyn Publications, 2009.

Belanger, Michelle. *Psychic Vampire Codex: A Manual of Magick and Energy Work.* Red Wheel/Weiser, LLC, 2004.

Belanger, Michelle. *The Ghost Hunter's Survival Guide: Personal Protection Techniques for Encounters with the Paranormal.* Llewellyn Publications, 2009.

Bible Gateway. Job 41. 2016. https://www.biblegateway.com/passage/?search=Job+41

Bible Hub. *Matthew.* 2016. http://biblehub.com/matthew/7-7.htm

Bodine, Echo. *Relax, It's Only a Ghost.* Element Books Ltd. 2000.

Briggs, Constance Victoria. *Encyclopedia of the Unseen World: The Ultimate Guide to Apparitions, Death Bed Visions, Mediums, Shadow People, Wandering Spirits, and Much, Much More.* Red Wheel/Weiser, 2010.

Burney, Diane. *Spiritual Clearings: Sacred Practices to Release Negative Energy and Harmonize Your Life.* North Atlantic Books, 2010.

Byrne, Lorna. *A Message of Hope from the Angels.* Coronet. 2012.

Byrne, Lorna. *Angels in My Hair.* Random House Digital, Inc., 2009.

Catholic Answers. *Interview with an exorcist.* 2016. http://www.catholic.com/magazine/articles/interview-with-an-exorcist

Catholics United for The Faith. *Exorcism in the Catholic Church.* 2016. http://www.cuf.org/2014/07/exorcism-catholic-church/

CNN travel. Unearthing Shanghai's Nine Dragon Pillar. 2016. http://travel.cnn.com/shanghai/play/unearthing-shanghais-nine-dragon-pillar-509418/

Constantine. Dir. Francis Lawrence. Perf. Keanu Reeves, Rachel Weisz, Shia LaBeouf, and Tilda Swinton. Warner Bros. Pictures, 2005. Film.

Calabrese, Adrian. *Sacred Signs: Hear, See and Believe Messages from the Universe.* Llewellyn Publications, 2013.

Chaudhary, Sufian. *The World of Archangels.* Sufian Chaudhary. Sufian Chaudhary, 2013.

Davidson, Gustav. *Dictionary of Angels.* Free Press. 2016.

Davis, Wade. *The Rainbow and the Serpent.* Simon and Schuster. 2010.

Denver Zombie Crawl. Denver Zombie Crawl. 2016. http://denverzombiecrawl.com

Dionysius the Areopagite. *The Celestial Hierarchy.* n.d.

Djinn Universe. *Types of Djinn.* 2016. http://www.djinnuniverse.com/types-of-djinn

Earth Witchery. *Faery.* 2016. http://www.earthwitchery.com/faery.htmls

Exemplore. *Fairy Dictionary A-Z of Fairies and the Wee Folk.* https://exemplore.com/magic/Fairy-Dictionary-A-Z-of-Fairies-and-the-Wee-Folk

Faerie Magick. *Faerie Likes and Dislikes.* 2016. http://faeriemagick.com/faeries-likes-and-dislikes/

Gehayi. *Writing Research Witch Trials The Great Witch.* 2016. http://gehayi.tumblr.com/post/140746528416/writing-research-witch-trials-the-great-witch

Gizmodo. *How a Zombie Outbreak Could Happen in Real Life?* 2016. http://io9.gizmodo.com/5916048/how-a-zombie-outbreak-could-happen-in-real-life

Godfrey, Linda. *Real Wolfmen True Encounters in Modern America.* Tarcher Perigee. 2012.

Goodreads. Elbert Hubbard Quotes. 2016. https://www.goodreads.com/quotes/138793-the-supernatural-is-the-natural-not-yet-understood

Greer, John Michael. *The New Encyclopedia of the Occult.* Llewellyn Publications, 2003.

Guiley, Rosemary Ellen. *The Djinn Connection.* Visionary Living, Inc. 2014.

Guiley, Rosemary Ellen. *The Encyclopedia of Angels.* Facts on File. 2004.

Guiley, Rosemary Ellen. *The Encyclopedia of Demons and Demonology.* Checkmark Books. 2009.

Guiley, Rosemary Ellen. *The Vengeful Djinn.* Llewellyn Publications. 2011.

Gregg, Susan. *Encyclopedia of Angels, Spirit Guides, and Ascended Masters: A Guide to 200 Celestial Beings.* Fair Winds Press, 2011.

Hill, Napoleon. *Outwitting the Devil.* Sterling Publishing. 2011.

IMDB. *Aladdin.* 2016. http://www.imdb.com/title/tt0103639/

IMDB. *Dawn of the Dead.* 2016. http://www.imdb.com/title/tt0077402/

IMDB. *Day of the Dead.* 2016. http://www.imdb.com/title/tt0088993/

IMDB. *Hotel Transylvania.* 2016. http://www.imdb.com/title/tt0837562/fullcredits/

IMDB. *I Dream of Jeannie.* http://www.imdb.com/title/tt0058815/?ref_=nv_sr_1

IMDB. *Insidious: Chapter 2.* 2016. http://www.imdb.com/title/tt2226417/

IMDB. *Night of the Living Dead.* 2016. http://www.imdb.com/title/tt0063350/

IMDB. *Return of the Living Dead.* 2016. http://www.imdb.com/title/tt0089907/

IMDB. *Seventh Son*. 2016.
http://www.imdb.com/title/tt1121096/quotes

IMDB. *Shaun of the Dead*. 2016.
http://www.imdb.com/title/tt0365748/

IMDB. *Supernatural*. 2016.
http://www.imdb.com/title/tt0460681/

IMDB. *The Walking Dead*. 2016.
http://www.imdb.com/title/tt1520211/

IMDB. *Underworld*. 2016.
http://www.imdb.com/title/tt0320691/

IMDB. *The Vampire Diaries*. 2016.
http://www.imdb.com/title/tt1405406/

IMDB. *Vampire Academy*. 2016.
http://www.imdb.com/title/tt1686821/

IMDB. *White Zombie*. 2016.
http://www.imdb.com/title/tt0023694/

IMDB. *World War Z*. 2016.
http://www.imdb.com/title/tt0816711/

IMDB. *Z Nation*. 2016. http://www.imdb.com/title/tt3843168/

Konstantinos. *Werewolves: The Occult Truth*. Llewellyn Publications. 2010.

Live Science. *Dragons*. 2016.
http://www.livescience.com/25559-dragons.html

Live Science. *Vampires Real History*. 2016. http://www.livescience.com/24374-vampires-real-history.html

MacKenzie, Shawn. *Dragons for Beginners: Ancient Creatures in a Modern World*. Llewellyn Publications. 2012.

McKinnin, F.J., *Befriending faeries: A Detailed Guide to Connect with Nature Spirits*. Niniane Press. 2013.

Mysterious Universe. The Mysterious Real Zombies of Haiti. 2016. http://mysteriousuniverse.org/2014/08/the-mysterious-real-zombies-of-haiti/

NAET. *Nambudripad's Allergy Elimination Techniques*. 2016. https://www.naet.com/

National Geographic. *World War Z, Could a Zombie Virus Happen ?*. 2016. http://voices.nationalgeographic.com/2013/06/25/world-war-z-could-a-zombie-virus-happen/

Nyland, A. Angels, Archangels, and Angel Categories: What the Ancients Said. Smith and Stirling, 2010.

On Century Avenue. *Shanghai Urban Legends*. 2016. http://oncenturyavenue.org/2014/10/shanghai-urban-legends/

Popular Science. *Could scientists really create zombie apocalypse virus?* 2016. http://www.popsci.com/science/article/2011-02/fyi-could-scientists-really-create-zombie-apocalypse-virus

Powers, Laura. *Angels: How to Understand, Recognize, and Receive Their Guidance*. Laura Powers Publishing, 2013.

Powers, Laura. *Angels and Manifesting*. Laura Powers Publishing, 2016.

Powers, Laura. *Life and the After-Life: Notes from a Medium and Angel Communicator*, Laura Powers Publishing, 2012.

Powers, Laura. *Diary of a Ghost Whisperer*. Laura Powers Publishing, 2015.

Powers, Laura. *Diary of a Psychic*. Laura Powers Publishing, 2016.

Praesidium of Warriors of St. Michael. *Stages of Demonic Influence*. 2016. http://pwsm-ri.org/Demonology/Stages-of-Demonic%20Influence.html

Prince, Derek. *They Shall Expel Demons*. Amazon Digital Services. 1998.

Sacred Texts. *The Book of Enoch*. 2016. http://www.sacred-texts.com/bib/boe/

Sacred Wicca. Faeries. 2016. http://sacredwicca.jigsy.com/faeries

Smithsonian. The Great New England Vampire Panic. 2016. http://www.smithsonianmag.com/history/the-great-new-england-vampire-panic-36482878/

Steiger, Brad. T*he Werewolf Book: The Encyclopedia of Shape-Shifting Beings*. Visible Ink Press, 2nd edition. 2011.

Summit Light House. *Elementals Nature Spirits*. 2016. http://www.summitlighthouse.org/elementals-nature-spirits/

Taylor, Sharae. *Archangels List.* 2016. www.angelsbysharae.com/Archangelslist.html

Urban Dictionary. *Ultra terrestrial.* 2016. http://www.urbandictionary.com/define.php?term=Ultraterrestrial

Thesaurus.com. *Ghost.* 2016. http://www.thesaurus.com/browse/ghost

Variety. *Guillermo Del Toro.* 2016. http://variety.com/2016/film/news/guillermo-del-toro-monsters-lacma-exhibit-1201827179/

Virtue, Doreen. *Angel Numbers 101: The Meaning of 111, 123, 444, and Other Number Sequences.* Hay House Inc., 2008.

Virtue, Doreen. *Archangels 101.* Hay House Inc., 2010.

Virtue, Doreen. *Archangels and Ascended Masters.* Hay House Inc., 2004.

Virtue, Doreen. *Earth Angels.* Hay House, 2002.

Virtue, Doreen. *Fairies 101: An Introduction to Connecting, Working, and Healing with the Fairies.* Hay House Inc., 2007.

Virtue, Doreen. *Goddesses and Angels.* Hay House Inc., 2006.

Virtue, Doreen. *Realms of the Earth Angels.* Hay House Inc., 2007.

Virtue, Doreen. *Solomon's Angels.* Hay House Inc., 2008.

Virtue, Doreen. *The Healing Miracles of the Archangel Raphael.* Hay House Inc., 2010.

Virtue, Doreen. *The Lightworkers Way*. Hay House Inc., 1997

Virtue, Doreen. *The Miracles of Archangel Michael*. Hay House Inc., 2008.

Van Praagh, James. *Ghosts Among Us*. Harper Collins, 2008.

Webster, Richard. *The Encyclopedia of Angels*. Llewellyn Publications. 2009.

What's Your Sign. *Chinese Dragons*. 2016. http://www.whats-your-sign.com/Chinese-dragons.html

What's Your Sign. *Sylphs Air Elementals*. 2016. http://www.whats-your-sign.com/sylphs-air-elementals.html

Wikipedia. *Book of Enoch*. 2016.
https://en.wikipedia.org/wiki/Book_of_Enoch

Wikipedia. *Book of Tobit*. 2016.
http://en.wikipedia.org/wiki/Book_of_Tobit

Wikipedia. *Bubonic Plague*. 2016.
https://en.m.wikipedia.org/wiki/Bubonic_plague

Wikipedia. *Cain and Able*. 2016.
https://en.wikipedia.org/wiki/Cain_and_Abel

Wikipedia. *Chinese Dragon*. 2016.
https://en.wikipedia.org/wiki/Chinese_dragon

Wikipedia. *Celestial Hierarchy*. 2016.
http://www.paranormality.com/celestial_hierarchy.shtml

Wikipedia. *Cryptid*. 2016.
https://en.wikipedia.org/wiki/Cryptid

Wikipedia. *Cryptozoology*. 2016.
https://en.wikipedia.org/wiki/Cryptozoology

Wikipedia. *Demonic Possession*. 2016.
https://en.wikipedia.org/wiki/Demonic_possession

Wikipedia. *Devil*. 2016. http://en.wikipedia.org/wiki/Devil

Wikipedia. *Electronic Voice Phenomenon*. 2016.
http://en.wikipedia.org/wiki/Electronic_voice_phenomenon

Wikipedia. *Gabriel*. 2016. http://en.wikipedia.org/wiki/Gabriel

Wikipedia. *Guillermo Del Toro*. 2016.
https://en.m.wikipedia.org/wiki/Guillermo_del_Toro

Wikipedia. *I am Legend*. 2016.
https://en.wikipedia.org/wiki/I_Am_Legend_(novel)

Wikipedia. *Ifrit*. 2016. https://en.m.wikipedia.org/wiki/Ifrit

Wikipedia. *Jiangshi*. 2016.
https://en.m.wikipedia.org/wiki/Jiangshi

Wikipedia. *Jinn*. 2016. https://en.wikipedia.org/wiki/Jinn

Wikipedia. *Leviathan*. 2016.
https://en.wikipedia.org/wiki/Leviathan

Wikipedia. *List of Beings Referred to as Faeries*. 2016.
https://en.m.wikipedia.org/wiki/List_of_beings_referred_to_as_fairies

Wikipedia. *List of Dragons in Mythology and Folklore*. 2016. https://en.wikipedia.org/wiki/List_of_dragons_in_mythology_and_folklore

Wikipedia. *List of Zombie Movies*. 2016. https://en.m.wikipedia.org/wiki/List_of_zombie_films

Wikipedia. *Marid*. 2016. https://en.m.wikipedia.org/wiki/Marid

Wikipedia. *Miracle*. 2016. http://en.wikipedia.org/wiki/Miracle

Wikipedia. *Mothman*. 2016. https://en.m.wikipedia.org/wiki/Mothman

Wikipedia. *Muhammed in Islam*. 2016. https://en.wikipedia.org/wiki/Muhammad_in_Islam

Wikipedia. *One Thousand and One Nights*. 2016. https://en.wikipedia.org/wiki/One_Thousand_and_One_Nights

Wikipedia. *Paranormal*. 2016. http://en.wikipedia.org/wiki/Paranormal

Wikipedia. *Qareen*. 2016. https://en.m.wikipedia.org/wiki/Qareen

Wikipedia. *Quran*. 2016. https://en.wikipedia.org/wiki/Quran

Wikipedia. *Richard Matheson*. 2016. https://en.wikipedia.org/wiki/Richard_Matheson

Wikipedia. *Salvia*. 2015. http://en.wikipedia.org/wiki/Salvia_officinalis

Wikipedia. *Salvia Apiana*. 2015.
http://en.wikipedia.org/wiki/Salvia_apiana

Wikipedia. *Seraphim*. 2016.
http://en.wikipedia.org/wiki/Christian_angelic_hierarchy#Seraphim

Wikipedia. *Skinwalker Ranch*. 2016.
https://en.m.wikipedia.org/wiki/Skinwalker_Ranch

Wikipedia. *Smudge Stick*. 2015.
http://en.wikipedia.org/wiki/Smudge_stick

Wikipedia. *Solomon*. 2016.
https://en.wikipedia.org/wiki/Solomon

Wikipedia. *Strigoi*. 2016. https://en.m.wikipedia.org/wiki/Strigoi

Wikipedia. *Vampire*. 2016.
https://en.m.wikipedia.org/wiki/Vampire

Wikipedia. *Vampire Hunter*. 2016.m
https://en.m.wikipedia.org/wiki/Vampire_hunter

Wikipedia. *Vrykolakas*. 2016.
https://en.m.wikipedia.org/wiki/Vrykolakas

Wikispaces.com. *Witch Hunts of Renaissance Europe*. 2016.
https://hysteriasinhistoryperiod2.wikispaces.com/Witch+Hunts+of+Renaissance+Europe

Wikipedia. *Zombie*. 2016.
https://en.m.wikipedia.org/wiki/Zombie

Wikipedia. *Zombie Walk*. 2016. https://en.m.wikipedia.org/wiki/Zombie_walk

Winkowski, Mary Ann. *When Ghosts Speak*. Grand Central Publishing, 2007.

Warren, Ed and Loraine. *Ghost Hunters*. Gramalkin Media. 2014.

Stay tuned for more information on Laura's upcoming book on Archangels and Ascended Masters.

For additional information on Laura's psychic work, go to www.healingpowers.net, you can sign up for her monthly newsletter to receive updates about Laura's books, speaking engagements, events, media and more.

About the Author – Laura Powers

Laura is a medium, angel communicator, ghost whisperer, actress, singer, model, and author of *Life and the After Life – Notes from a Medium and Angel Communicator; Angels: How to Understand, Recognize, and Receive their Guidance; Diary of a Ghost Whisperer; Angels and Manifesting;* and *Diary of a Psychic.* She received her bachelor's degree in theatre and her master's degree in political science from the University of Colorado. When she is not writing or traveling, you may find her singing, dancing, or exploring the unknown. You can find more information about her acting, singing and fiction writing on her website www.laurapowers.net. You can find more information about her work in this field on the website www.healingpowers.net. Laura is currently working on her next book as well as a screenplay and a television show inspired by her life as a psychic.

www.ingramcontent.com/pod-product-compliance
Lightning Source LLC
Chambersburg PA
CBHW060147100426
42744CB00007B/935